A Taste of Summer

A Taste of Summer

Beverley Sutherland Smith

photography by Ray Joyce

Salem House Publishers

Topsfield, Massachusetts

DEDICATION

For Gwenda Bailey, Marie Stephens, Betty Campbell and Barbara
Killeen, who throughout past years have given such invaluable
help in the kitchen.

ACKNOWLEDGEMENTS

The Publishers would like to thank Matchbox shops, Melbourne,
Pino Narduzzo and George Tumino for their assistance in
supplying food and props for photography.

First published in the United States
by Salem House Publishers, 1987,
462 Boston Street, Topsfield, MA 01983

Published by Lansdowne Press, Sydney
a division of RPLA Pty Limited
176 South Creek Road, Dee Why West, N.S.W. Australia, 2099

Copyright Beverley Sutherland Smith 1983

Produced in Australia by the Publisher
Typeset in Australia at Griffin Press Limited, Adelaide
Printed in Hong Kong by Dainippon Printing Co. (HK) Ltd.
Managing Editor: Susan Tomnay
Editor: Doreen Grézoux
Designer: Elaine Rushbrooke

Library of Congress Catalog Card Number: 86-63106

ISBN 0 88162 233 8

Previous page
Prosciutto with melon
(page 53)

Contents

Introduction

According to the gastronomic dictionary, *Larousse Gastronomique*, salads are 'Dishes made up of herbs, plants, vegetables, eggs, meat and fish, seasoned with oil, vinegar, salt and pepper, with or without other ingredients.'

Until some years ago *salad* in America meant a collection of ingredients which mostly consisted of lettuce, some processed cheese either grated or cut into strips, a piece of sliced tomato usually under-ripe and inevitably a thick piece of beetroot. A sad miserable concoction.

If there is one particular dish which would indicate the changed sophistication of the American palate it is in the vast and interesting collections of salads which are served now, whether for first courses, main dishes or as an accompaniment.

Presentation is of vital importance with a salad; since cold food doesn't offer much to our sense of smell, we must rely on a visually pleasing arrangement to excite our taste buds.

If there was one particular influence in creating this book, it came from the ingredients themselves. While some ideas were prompted by memories of wonderful meals I have eaten in many different parts of the world, and others by skimming through books, it was the variety of produce from the local markets and my own garden which supplied the most inspiration.

New potatoes, waxy and with a papery, transparent skin, sun-ripened sweet tomatoes, a bunch of feathery chervil or some large perfumed leaves of basil, all very simple things but their freshness makes the difference between a synthetic manufactured taste and that of real food, a difference which makes cooking and eating such a joy. It may be possible with cooked food to sometimes disguise inferior ingredients with a rich sauce, a strong tasting stuffing or a medley of ingredients which can confuse the palate, but the standard of a salad is based without question on the quality of the raw produce.

Quantities

All these recipes serve four people unless otherwise specified. However I do concede that the portions are small. I prefer to eat small portions and find a heaped plate unpleasant and it usually results in an instant loss of appetite.

Obviously however you must use your own judgement as it is a matter of personal taste and depends greatly on individual appetites and on what else is served at dinner. This entire question as to how much will serve how many was answered beautifully in a quote which has been attributed to that writer and gourmet, the late Alice B. Toklas. When asked how many each of her recipes would serve she replied, 'How can I tell how hungry your guests will be when they sit down to dine.'

Oils

Hazelnut Oil

Safflower Oil

Virgin Olive Oil

Sunflower Oil

Sesame Oil

Peanut Oil

Pure Olive Oil

Garlic/Herb Olive Oil

Grape Seed Oil

Walnut Oil

Vinegars

Spiced mint vinegar

Lemon vinegar

Raspberry vinegar (2)

Lavender vinegar

Basil vinegar made
with red basil

Lemon and spearmint vinegar

Tarragon vinegar

Thyme vinegar made
with lemon thyme

Borage vinegar

Basil vinegar made
with green basil

Rosemary vinegar

Celery vinegar

Raspberry vinegar (1)

Garlic vinegar made
with red wine vinegar

Dressings

Dressing with Egg

Spiced dressing

Anchovy dressing with olives and pimento

Blue Cheese dressing

Egg mayonnaise (whole egg)

Mayonnaise (egg yolk)

Boiled mayonnaise

Dressing with fresh herbs

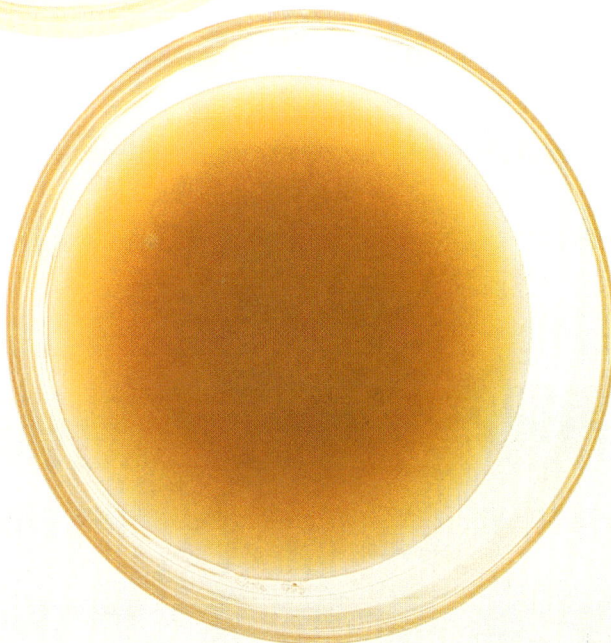

Dressing with Anchovy

13

Herbs

Green Basil

Salad Burnet

Chives

Borage

Dill

Chervil

Lemon Thyme

Red Basil

Garden Thyme

Nasturtium

Vietnamese Mint

Curly Mint

Coriander

Flat Parsley

Tarragon

Rosemary

Curly Parsley

15

Salad Ingredients

Tomato

**Cherry
Tomatoes**

Tomato

**Yellow Zucchini
(Courgette)**

Zucchini (Courgette)

Baby Squash

Spanish Onion

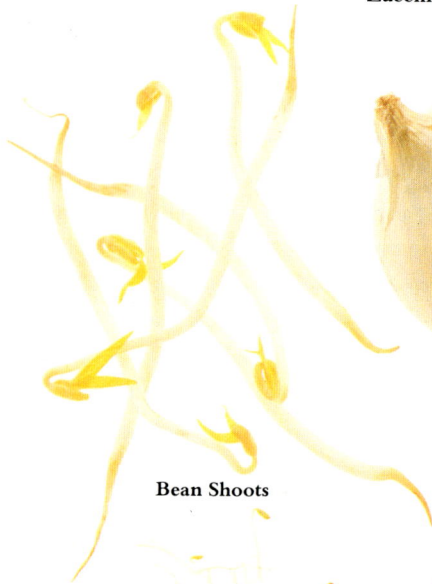

White Onion

Brown Onion

Bean Shoots

Shallot

Alfalfa

Garlic

Root Ginger

**Spring Onion
(Scallion)**

Yellow Pepper
(Capsicum)

Sweet Yellow
Pepper

Green Pepper
(Capsicum)

Red Pepper
(Capsicum)

Peas

Snow Peas
(Mange Tout)

Green Chilli

Red Chilli

Mushrooms

Radish

Witlof (Endive/Chicory)

White Radish

Eggplant (Aubergine)

17

Salad Ingredients

Mignonette Lettuce

Iceberg Lettuce

Raddichio

Spinach

Endive (Chicory)

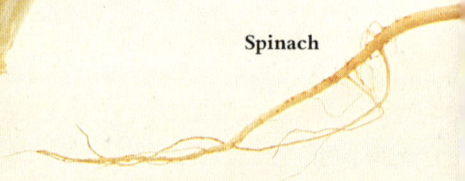

Butter Lettuce

Watercress

Cress

Cos Lettuce

Sorrel

Salad Preparation

Salad Bowls

In the past wooden bowls were the main type used for serving salad at the table. Nowadays glass, china or plastic are more popular.

Clear bowls are particularly attractive, since you can see the colour and beauty of the salad from all sides, not just from the top.

One of the problems with wooden bowls is that with use some become slightly rancid from the oils and garlic. If you have a wooden bowl which you would still care to maintain, try cleaning it by rubbing the inside with lemon juice and then coarse salt. Rinse and leave to dry and repeat several times. If the oil has soaked deeply into the wood though, it is almost impossible to clean.

Lettuce Preparation

There are differing opinions as to whether lettuce should be cut with a knife or torn for salads.

Personally I prefer to tear them for a mixed salad but it does not matter a great deal provided care is taken. Cutting, except with stainless steel, begins an oxidation process which causes the cut edge to darken but as lettuce is generally used fairly quickly afterwards this does not matter unless it is stored for some time.

Storing Lettuce

There is a variety of containers available on the market for keeping lettuce crisp. But since they vary so much in price and in the results they achieve, we concentrated, while working on this book on the ways of storing lettuce that didn't require buying bowls or containers specially made for the purpose.

The lettuce was checked each day to try to determine the simplest way to keep it fresh. Obviously the sooner you can use the lettuce after buying it, the better, but this may not always be possible.

1. Unwashed lettuce, placed in a plastic bag and refrigerated in the vegetable crisper gradually became wilted and the outside leaves had to be discarded after 3 to 4 days.

2. Lettuce, washed and carefully separated, then dried and stored in a plastic bag, became crisp and kept well for about 4 days but gradually began to brown on the stalk ends.

3. Best of all: washed lettuce leaves, carefully separated and dried, then lightly wrapped in a tea towel and placed in the crisper, were still fresh after 5 to 7 days.

There are also appliances available which remove moisture quickly and easily from washed lettuce.

A plastic container which has a rapid, spinning action is marketed for this purpose. But of course lettuce can be quite easily dried by gently and carefully patting with kitchen paper towels or soft tea towels.

Although the outside leaves should be washed and so should the root end, which may be sandy or gritty, the tightly curled inner part which is not exposed to handling needs little water, except perhaps a rinse at the end of the stalks.

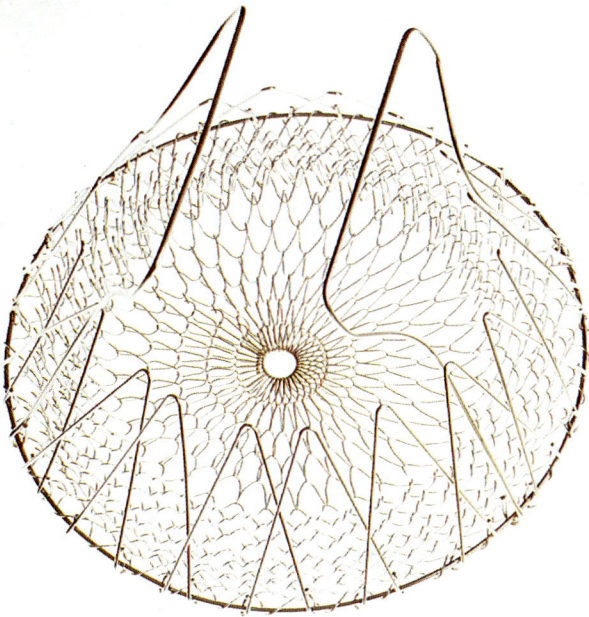

Wire drainer

Teatowel storage

Separated, washed lettuce,
stored in plastic bag

Whole lettuce in bag

First Courses

Tomato and Egg salad with Nasturtium Leaves

Baby nasturtium leaves are folded over a cream cheese filling which has been mixed with some finely chopped fresh herbs. Don't be deterred by the unusual combination, the bite of the nasturtium leaf is wonderful with the richness of the cheese. Arranged over the top of the tomato and egg salad it has a summery look and a fresh taste.

If you don't have nasturtium leaves, mound some of the cheese in the centre of the salad and surround it with the sliced tomato and egg.

Serves 4

125 g (4 oz) cream cheese (see note)
18 to 24 small nasturtium leaves
salt and pepper
1 tablespoon finely chopped chives
2 tablespoons finely chopped fresh chervil
1 teaspoon paprika
500 g (1 lb) tomatoes, peeled
2 tablespoons finely chopped fresh basil
sugar
4 hard-boiled eggs

Note: Buy a fresh cream cheese, if you can obtain it, rather than one with gum additives, which will make a much heavier filling.

Dressing:
4 tablespoons vegetable or olive oil
1 tablespoon white wine vinegar

Prepare the cream cheese first as it needs to be chilled before it is served.

Mash the cheese thoroughly with the chives, chervil and paprika and season with salt and pepper.

Wash the leaves and pat them dry. Place a small teaspoonful of the cream cheese on one side of each leaf and fold the leaf over. They will stick together easily.

Refrigerate, covered, for about an hour or until the cheese filling is firm.

Cut the tomatoes into thin slices and place half in a layer on a platter. Scatter a little basil on top and season each slice with salt and a pinch of sugar.

Slice the eggs thinly and arrange half over the tomato. Repeat with the remaining tomato and egg.

Whisk the oil and vinegar and scatter over the top. Once the dressing is added don't leave the salad for more than an hour or it will become too wet.

Serve with the filled nasturtium leaves arranged over the top.

Egg salad with Olive dressing

The history of the olive dates back into antiquity and it is even mentioned in the Bible. Apart from the pungent flavour of the olive, it has always been highly valued for its oil and, in the countries where it grows prolifically, the tree signifies peace and good fortune.

There are many types of olives, in all sizes and in many different colours, from the small, wrinkled, salty olives to the grand, smooth huge ones, ranging in colour from a creamy chocolate to green, mauve, brown or purple.

The choice of olive is dependent not only on personal taste but on the way you intend to use it. For this dish I prefer to use a plain green olive, the type with a stone. It is well flavoured but not too salty or strong. You can buy small, stoned olives in jars and these could be used if you wish to save time. However, avoid the very large stoned olives because even though they look magnificent, they don't have as much flavour.

This olive dressing is perfect as a first course served with hard-boiled eggs.

Serves 4

Olive Dressing:
$\frac{3}{4}$ cup green olives (with stones)
$\frac{1}{4}$ cup (2 fl oz) vegetable oil
$\frac{1}{3}$ cup (2$\frac{1}{2}$ fl oz) mayonnaise
2 tablespoons cream
2 teaspoons grated onion
few drops Tabasco

Salad:
6 hard-boiled eggs
6 green olives

For this dish, it is best to prepare the dressing first so that it can be chilled for a short time before using. The hard-boiled eggs can be sliced shortly before serving time.

To make the dressing, place the olives in a pan of cold water. Bring the water to the boil and immediately drain.

Cut the olives away from the stone. Place the pieces, with the oil, into a food processor or blender and process to a fine purée.

Gently stir in the mayonnaise, cream, onion and Tabasco. The mixture will be quite thick; if you prefer a thinner mixture use a little extra cream.

Taste, and add seasoning if necessary, although the olives should provide plenty of salt.

To assemble the salad, place a spoonful of dressing on individual plates and spread out in a thin layer.

Cut the eggs into thin slices and arrange overlapping slices on the dressing. Spoon a little mound of dressing in the centre, but leave some of the egg showing.

Cut the olive flesh from the stones and then cut into fine strips. Sprinkle over the centre of the salad.

Eggs with Mushrooms

The eggs have a lightly-curried mushroom filling and the accompanying mushroom salad is also curry-flavoured.

Although the egg is rich, the salad is light, and the tartness of the lemon prevents it from being too heavy for a first course.

Serves 6

6 hard-boiled eggs
1 tablespoon finely chopped shallots (or spring onions)
1 tablespoon vegetable oil
185 g (6 oz) mushrooms, finely diced
salt and pepper
2 teaspoons Madras curry powder, or to taste
cream

Mushroom salad:
185 g (6 oz) small firm white mushrooms
2 tablespoons lemon juice
2 tablespoons finely chopped parsley
salt and pepper

To finish the salad:
6 lettuce leaves
3 tablespoons mayonnaise
3 tablespoons cream

Cut the hard-boiled eggs in half lengthwise and remove the yolks. Place these into a bowl and mash finely.

Place the shallots and oil into a frying pan, sauté for a few seconds and then add the mushrooms. (These need to be finely diced or they won't mix evenly with the egg yolks.)

Fry quickly until the mushrooms have softened. Season with salt and pepper. It is best to keep the heat high so that they don't stew.

Add the curry powder, stir to heat through and remove from the heat. The curry should be spicy but not too hot so use your judgement as to whether to use more than the two teaspoons of powder, or less.

Mix the mushrooms into the egg and mash well, adding enough cream to make a soft paste.

Check for seasoning and pack a generous amount of the filling back into the egg white halves.

Cover and refrigerate if not using immediately but allow them to return to room temperature for one hour before using, as chilling dulls the flavour.

Mushroom salad: Remove the stalks from the mushrooms. Don't peel the caps but either wipe or wash them.

Cut the mushrooms into wafer-thin slices and place into a bowl. Add the lemon juice, parsley, salt and pepper. Stir to mix the lemon through and allow to stand for one hour.

The mushrooms will become softer; there shouldn't be too much liquid but if there is drain some of it away before assembling the salad.

To finish the salad: Shred the lettuce finely and place along the centre of an oval platter. Arrange the eggs, filled side down, in a row on the lettuce. Spoon the mushroom salad on either side of the eggs.

Mix together the mayonnaise and cream. Spoon a little over each egg, first wiping the tops of the eggs to remove any moisture otherwise the mayonnaise will slide off.

Once you have prepared the salad to this stage, serve within half an hour.

Salad St Tropez

Naming this salad after the small French fishing village of St Tropez is more wistful remembrance than anything else, because I don't recollect eating one like this while I was there.

However, I do remember that in the little market at the back of the shops one could buy the best marinated peppers I have ever tasted. All different colours, they were prepared locally and scooped out of a tall glass jar, the peppers glistening with oil and smoky in flavour. A thick layer, placed inside a long French bread stick, made the most delicious lunch imaginable.

This salad of sautéed small mushrooms has a rich, pepper taste and is aromatic and rustic. It is good enough to eat on its own with some bread or serve alongside a simple steak dish.

Serves 4

1 tablespoon vegetable oil
1 large white onion, cut in half and sliced thinly
375 g (12 oz) small button mushrooms
45 g (1½ oz) butter
1 clove garlic, crushed
salt and pepper
1 tablespoon lemon juice
3 medium-sized yellow peppers (capsicums)
3 medium-sized red peppers (capsicums)

3 medium-sized green peppers (capsicums)

Dressing:
1 tablespoon finely chopped anchovy fillets
1 clove garlic, crushed
pepper
1 teaspoon tomato purée
1 teaspoon sugar
3 tablespoons olive oil
1 tablespoon white wine vinegar

Heat the oil in a frying pan and add the onion slices. Sauté gently until slightly softened, stirring occasionally. Don't let them become too soft, some firm texture is good. Remove to a bowl.

Remove the stalks from the mushrooms, if they are woody, and cut the mushrooms in half.

Into the same pan, place the mushrooms, butter and garlic, season with salt and pepper and toss for a couple of minutes until softened. Mix the mushrooms with the onion. Season with the lemon juice.

Cut the peppers in half and remove the seeds. Press them down a little to flatten them so they will grill (broil) evenly.

Place the peppers under the griller and let them cook until the skins are blistered and dark brown. Remove and leave to cool slightly, so they can be handled easily. Peel away the skin, which will be like tissue paper, and cut the peppers into thick strips.

Place the mushrooms in a mound in the centre of a platter. You can arrange the peppers in two ways; either mix them together lightly with two forks, or arrange them in separate coloured bundles around the mushrooms.

To make the dressing, crush the anchovy fillets with a fork, add the garlic, pepper, tomato purée, sugar, olive oil and vinegar. Whisk with a fork until the dressing is thick. (It can be made beforehand, but stir well again before using.)

Spoon the dressing over the peppers only, not the mushrooms, and serve.

The peppers can be prepared the previous day and, even with dressing over them, they will keep beautifully if covered and refrigerated. Remove from the refrigerator about 1 hour before serving.

Eggs with Mushrooms (page 24)

Egg Mayonnaise salad (page 112)

Tomato and Egg salad with Nasturtium Leaves (page 24)

Sliced Avocado with Walnut dressing

A perfect, ripe avocado served with a dressing makes a deliciously simple, albeit slightly rich, first course. The most usual accompaniment is a vinaigrette dressing made from oil and vinegar.

This dressing contains walnuts and is extraordinarily good, although there are a few points to remember. If the walnuts are not really sweet and fresh, and in the packets they sometimes become stronger flavoured and almost bitter, use freshly cracked walnuts. The sweeter the flavour, the nicer the dish. You will only need a few walnuts so the task of cracking them is not tedious.

Despite care, avocado does darken as it stands so cut it as near to serving time as possible. However, the dressing can be made several hours beforehand and then stirred again before using.

Some walnut oil is used in the dressing along with a lighter oil. The combination is better than using only walnut, which becomes too overpowering for the avocado flavour.

Serves 4
**2 medium-sized ripe
  avocados
4 walnut halves
watercress or parsley
  (optional)**

Dressing:
½ cup (2 oz) walnuts

**1 clove garlic, crushed
2 tablespoons walnut oil
4 tablespoons peanut or
  light vegetable oil
2 tablespoons lemon juice
1 tablespoon white wine
  vinegar
salt
white pepper**

Cut the avocados in half and twist them to remove the stone. Peel and cut each half into thin slices.

Arrange the slices in a fan shape on individual plates. Coat with the dressing, leaving some of the avocado showing.

To make the dressing, grind the walnuts, but don't let the mixture become mealy; there should be just a little texture remaining. You can cut them up by hand, if you wish, making the mixture very fine so the flavour will be released into the dressing.

Mix the garlic into the walnuts, gradually adding the walnut oil, peanut or vegetable oil, lemon juice, vinegar and salt and pepper. The dressing will be very thick.

Arrange a walnut half on each serving at the narrow part of the fan. You can use a sprig of watercress or flat leaf parsley for decoration, if you wish, to give additional colour.

Tomato and Mozzarella

Italian mozzarella cheese was once made exclusively from buffalo's milk, but now it is made from cow's milk. Like so many classic cheeses it is widely imitated in other countries and its use in cooking is largely due to its melting qualities.

The mozzarella used in this salad is not the firm, factory-made product but fresh mozzarella. It is roughly ball-shaped, made in the traditional method, moist and dripping with whey.

You may wonder what is the use of all this if it is not easily obtainable and, admittedly, it is not a cheese to be found in a supermarket. But each city with an Italian community will nearly always have shops that sell the fresh product. It is worth looking for. Combined in this salad it has a wonderful pungent taste, blending with fresh ripe tomatoes and the perfume of basil.

Serves 4
**4 small ripe tomatoes
2-4 mozzarella cheeses
  (bocconcini) depending
  on size**

Dressing:
**3 tablespoons olive oil
1 tablespoon lemon juice
2 tablespoons basil leaves**

Wash the tomatoes but don't peel them. Cut into thin slices, keeping them together so you can reshape the tomatoes.

Cut the mozzarella into thin slices. When you buy the cheese you will need to judge how many are required by their size since they can vary. Each slice of tomato has alongside it a slice of mozzarella.

Arrange on individual plates alternating slices of tomato and cheese, packing them tightly together to form a long roll. Allow 1 tomato and about half a cheese per person.

Pour the dressing over the top. To make the dressing, whisk the oil and lemon juice, or shake them in a jar. Break the basil leaves into tiny pieces and add.

The cheese and tomato can be assembled a little while beforehand but leave the dressing until serving time.

Decorate with a few fresh leaves of basil.

This is also good with a few pieces of anchovy on top, if you like it.

Mushrooms in Curry mayonnaise

If you buy tiny button mushrooms for this, they have a good texture but not a great deal of flavour so use ones which are firm but just starting to open slightly.

The caps usually only need to be wiped, but if they are gritty you may need to wash them carefully. Dry well before using in the salad.

It is quite a rich dish so a small serve is sufficient for a first course.

Serves 4
**1 tablespoon vegetable oil
1 medium-sized white
  onion, finely chopped
3 teaspoons curry powder
½ cup (4 fl oz) mayonnaise
1 tablespoon tomato sauce
  (ketchup)**

**375 g (12 oz) small button
  mushrooms
2 tablespoons slivered
  almonds
4 lettuce leaves**

Place the oil and onion in a frying pan and sauté, stirring occasionally, until the onion has softened. Add the curry powder and fry for a minute. Remove and leave to cool slightly.

Mix into the mayonnaise with the tomato sauce. You can prepare this hours beforehand but mix with the mushrooms only about 30 minutes to 1 hour before serving.

Cut the mushrooms stalks level with the caps. If tough and woody remove them completely. Slice very thinly and mix into the mayonnaise.

Cook the almonds in a dry frying pan until golden. Watch so they colour evenly, tossing with a fork. Leave to cool.

Place a lettuce leaf on each plate; try to use ones which have a cup shape. Spoon the mushroom mixture into the centre and scatter some almonds on top.

Tomato and Mozzarella (page 28)

Mushrooms in Curry mayonnaise (page 28)

Asparagus and Prawn salad

I like this made with prawns but you could use crayfish, crab or any shellfish. The salad has a lovely colour with the pink of the prawns, the creamy mushrooms and the bright green asparagus arranged in a random pattern on top.

For effect, it probably looks better on a large platter although it may be easier to serve if individual plates are used.

It is best assembled at the last moment but the mushrooms and prawns could be mixed together and the asparagus cooked several hours beforehand.

Serves 4
500 g (1 lb) asparagus
250 g (8 oz) tiny button mushrooms
milk
salt and pepper
500 g (1 lb) shelled prawns (small ones are better for this dish)
lettuce

Dressing:
4 tablespoons vegetable oil

1 tablespoon walnut oil (see note)
2 tablespoons lemon juice
1 tablespoon finely chopped shallots (spring onions)
salt and pepper
Note: The walnut oil does give a marvellous flavour to the salad but if you can't obtain this, use a little light olive oil in combination with the vegetable oil instead.

Break the asparagus stalks where they will bend easily. Peel them to just below the tips using a vegetable peeler or a small sharp knife.

Heat a frying pan, three-quarters full of salted water, and add the asparagus. Cook over high heat until just tender. They will keep firm when cooked in this way and there is no need to tie them in bundles. When ready, remove from the water and place into cold water to chill quickly so they stop cooking and remain bright green. Drain well before using.

Trim the stalks of the mushrooms level with the caps. Wipe the tops of the mushrooms. Place into a saucepan with sufficient milk to come about half-way up the mushrooms. Season with salt and pepper. Cook over gentle heat for about 10 minutes or until they have softened. Drain well.

Arrange sufficient lettuce leaves to cover the base of individual plates or a large platter.

Mix the prawns and mushrooms together and place on top of the lettuce. Arrange the asparagus over the top, rather like a lattice, so you can see the prawns through it.

To make the dressing, place the 2 oils in a basin and add the lemon, whisking so it thickens. Mix in the shallots and season. The dressing can be made well beforehand; just stir again before using.

Spoon the dressing over the entire salad and serve immediately.

Asparagus with Shreds of Egg

As a first course this amount of asparagus, combined with the egg, should be sufficient but it does depend on whether you lose some of the stalks in trimming, so use your own judgement. Even if you use more asparagus, don't alter the number of eggs because this amount is plenty for four.

The asparagus is mixed with dressing and the egg shreds rest lightly on top. As they have sufficient flavour of their own, add them at the last moment so they won't have any vinegar or oil mixed with them.

Serves 4
750 g (1½ lb) asparagus
salt
2 eggs
45 g (1½ oz) ham, finely diced (see note)
2 tablespoons finely chopped spring onions (Scallions)
2 tablespoons water
2 teaspoons soy sauce
pepper
oil
Note: It is important to cut

the ham very finely or you will not be able to shred the omelettes thinly. Instead, they will break into chunky pieces and although the taste will be good, the appearance will not be the same.

Dressing:
½ cup (4 fl oz) olive or vegetable oil
1 teaspoon Dijon mustard
2 tablespoons white wine vinegar

Break the asparagus where it bends easily. Trim away the outside skin to just below the tips. Heat some water in a frying pan and when boiling add the asparagus and some salt. Boil over a high heat until the asparagus is just barely tender. Cooked this way the stalks will be cooked but the tips will remain firm.

Drain and immediately run cold water over the asparagus to retain the bright green colour and prevent it cooking any further. Drain well.

Place into a shallow dish or on a plate which has a slight edge.

Mix together all the dressing ingredients and either whisk them or shake them in a jar until thickened.

Pour some of the dressing over the asparagus and leave to stand for about 30 minutes, or longer if necessary. Don't refrigerate it as this will spoil the flavour.

Beat the eggs with the ham, spring onions, water, soy sauce and pepper.

Heat sufficient oil to barely coat the base of a frying pan.

Pour in a little of the egg to form a very thin omelette, tilting the pan so that the egg covers the base.

Cook over a medium heat, just until the egg is set. Using a spatula, remove the omelette carefully and place on a board to cool.

Repeat until all the egg is used. You will probably have sufficient for 2 or 3 omelettes, depending on the size of your frying pan.

Roll the omelettes tightly and cut them into thin strips.

Arrange the asparagus on individual plates, fanning out the tips and trimming the ends slightly if necessary. Spoon a little more dressing over the asparagus to coat.

Arrange the omelette shreds across the stalks, leaving the tips showing, and serve immediately.

Asparagus with Egg and Ham

Asparagus has an affinity with egg and they are combined in many recipes, such as the Flemish mashed egg served mixed with melted butter, or in some of the sauces, such as Hollandaise, which have a rich butter and egg taste.

In this salad the egg is cold but mixed with mayonnaise.

The asparagus stalks are placed on top and the moist, well-flavoured mixture underneath acts as a sauce. There is no need for any dressing, which would conflict with the delicate flavours.

It is important, however, not to overcook the egg but to keep it creamy and light. If it is left just a few minutes too long in the pan it will become granulated and dry.

The dish is quite substantial so you will need only a light main course to follow.

If you add a little extra asparagus and another couple of eggs it could be served as the main dish for lunch or a light evening meal.

Serves 4
750 g (1½ lb) asparagus
4 eggs
2 tablespoons cream
1 tablespoon dry white wine
salt and pepper

45 g (1½ oz) butter
2 tablespoons mayonnaise
1 tablespoon finely chopped chives
60 g (2 oz) ham, cut in thin strips

Break the asparagus where it bends. Peel the stalk using a small sharp knife or a vegetable peeler to just below the tip.

Bring some water to the boil in a frying pan. Add the asparagus; there is no need to tie it in a bundle when cooking it this way. Salt the water and leave the asparagus to cook until just barely tender. Test with the point of a knife to check. Remove, drain and place into some cold water immediately to retain the bright green colour and stop it cooking any further. Drain well.

Beat the eggs with the cream, wine, salt and pepper. Melt the butter in a frying pan, add the eggs and cook until they are set but still creamy. Remove and place into a basin. Leave to cool and then add the mayonnaise and chives and taste for seasoning.

To serve: Place a flat layer of the egg on individual plates. Scatter with a little ham. Arrange the asparagus stalks on top, trimming the ends if they are too uneven.

The Flower salad

There are no flowers in this salad; it is given this name because of the presentation, which could be used for other dishes as well. A photograph of it appears on the front cover.

The leaves of English spinach are arranged in a petal form on a flat plate. Tiny mignonette lettuce leaves, with their paler green tinged with brown, are arranged in the centre of the plate and the salad is placed inside this to form the heart of the flower.

Dressing is not added to either the spinach or the lettuce because the salad will have sufficient.

This makes a generous amount as a first course and if you are having something substantial afterwards would easily extend to six people.

This salad contains a generous amount of protein so you may find it adequate for a light meal, or you could serve it with a side dish of egg salad.

Serves 4
250 g (8 oz) small new potatoes
125 g (4 oz) bacon, finely diced
1 small white onion, finely diced
2 tomatoes, about 375 g (12 oz) altogether, peeled
60 g (2 oz) Gruyère cheese, cut in small strips
1 medium-sized avocado
32 small English spinach leaves
16 baby mignonette lettuce leaves

Dressing:
½ cup (4 fl oz) vegetable or olive oil
2 tablespoons white vinegar or lemon juice
1 teaspoon dry, English-style mustard
1 teaspoon Dijon mustard
1 tablespoon finely chopped sweet-sour cucumber
salt and pepper

Cook the potatoes, in their jackets, in salted water until tender. Drain and when cool enough to handle, remove the skins. Cut into small dice.

Cook the bacon and onion in a frying pan, stir occasionally and when the bacon fat is transparent and the onion slightly softened, remove to kitchen paper to drain.

Chop the tomato into tiny dice, drain away some of the liquid and seeds.

You can prepare all these ingredients and mix them with the dressing, but leave the avocado until nearer to serving time so that it keeps its colour.

To make the dressing, place the oil and vinegar in a bowl, whisk with a fork, or shake together in a jar. Add the remaining ingredients and mix again. (This can be left to stand for some time but stir well before using.)

Mix everything well and about 30 minutes before serving dice the avocado and add.

Assemble the salad as described in the introduction to this recipe, with the spinach representing the petals of a flower and the mignonette leaves and salad the centre.

Asparagus with shreds of Egg (page 30)

Zucchini salad (page 125)

Bagatelle salad (page 44)

Tofu salad

Tofu, or soy bean curd as it is often known, has such importance for the people of Asia that it has been mentioned since earliest times in proverbs and poems.

Tofu is often called 'meat without a bone' because of its high protein content. Although it has little actual flavour, it has a smooth velvety texture which lends itself to a variety of dishes.

In this salad tofu is used in more a Western than an Oriental style. It is sold in a flat cake and can easily be obtained from Oriental shops or grocers. It is soft and fragile, so handle it carefully. If using within 24 hours, store it in a covered container in the refrigerator but if you intend keeping it longer, put it in a dish and cover with fresh water. Change the water daily and it will keep for a week.

Only a small amount is used in this salad; if you like you can easily double the amount.

Serves 4–6
1 small cucumber, about 250 g (8 oz)
salt and sugar
125 g (4 oz) tofu (bean curd)
1 large tomato, about 185 g (6 oz), peeled
2 tablespoons finely chopped spring onions (scallions)
2 tablespoons roughly chopped walnuts

4 large lettuce leaves (cup-shaped)

Dressing:
1 tablespoon soy sauce
1 teaspoon finely grated fresh ginger
1 tablespoon vegetable oil
few drops Tabasco
1 tablespoon lemon juice

To finish the salad:
2 tablespoons mayonnaise

Peel the cucumber and cut it in half lengthwise. Remove the seeds and cut the cucumber into small dice. Sprinkle with a little salt and sugar and leave to stand for about 30 minutes. Drain well.

Place the tofu on an oven tray and cook under the griller until the top is golden. Keep turning the tofu until all the outside is golden. Leave to cool a couple of minutes, then cut into chunky bite-sized pieces or strips.

Mix all the dressing ingredients together in a bowl. Whisk with a fork. It should not need any additional seasoning—the soy sauce will provide sufficient.

Place the tofu into a bowl and while it is slightly warm, mix in the dressing. You will need to do this part of the salad beforehand for the tofu to marinate. The remainder of the salad can either be prepared now and mixed through or left until later.

Cut the tomato into small dice, removing some of the seeds, and mix with the cucumber, tofu, chopped spring onions and walnuts. This can all be done several hours beforehand and the salad refrigerated if the day is warm.

Break any centre core from the lettuce leaves. Place some of the tofu salad in each cup of lettuce. Top with a little mayonnaise and serve immediately.

Eggplant and Tomato salad

This is a delightfully pungent salad of cooked eggplant coated with a layer of tomato. It could be part of an hors d'oeuvre platter or is very good served with some crusty bread as a first course, provided the remainder of the meal is well-flavoured otherwise the strong taste of this dish will make everything else appear rather bland.

If you are serving this as an accompaniment, it is best with barbecued or plainly cooked meat such as beef.

Use small eggplants rather than large ones. Sliced lengthwise the large eggplant will be awkward to handle and not look nearly so attractive for serving.

Serves 4
250 g (8 oz) small eggplants
salt
flour
vegetable or olive oil
250 g (8 oz) ripe tomatoes, peeled

Dressing:
1 clove garlic, crushed
1 tablespoon finely chopped parsley

$\frac{1}{2}$ cup (4 fl oz) olive oil
2 tablespoons red wine vinegar
1 tablespoon finely chopped capers
1 tablespoon finely chopped anchovy fillets
1 teaspoon tomato paste
$\frac{1}{2}$ teaspoon sugar
pepper

Remove both the stalk and the rounded end from the eggplants. Cut a thin slice from the side, lengthwise, and discard. Cut thin slices, again lengthwise, making about 4 from each eggplant.

Sprinkle lightly with salt and leave to stand for about 30 minutes. When wet on top, rinse the eggplant slices and pat them dry. Dust lightly with flour.

Heat sufficient oil to lightly coat the base of a frying pan. Add the eggplant and cook until golden on the outside and tender inside, turning once. If the eggplants are young, this should take only a few minutes each side. Place on kitchen paper to drain.

To make the dressing, mix the garlic and parsley, whisk in the oil and vinegar with a fork, add the capers, anchovy, tomato paste and sugar. Because of the salt in the anchovy this shouldn't need any more but you can be generous with the pepper.

Place the dressing in a shallow bowl. Dip the eggplant slices lightly into the dressing so that the outside is coated and then place them on a flat platter.

Cut the tomato into thin slices. Put them into the same pan in which the eggplant was cooked and fry them for a couple of seconds on each side.

Remove from the pan and place on the slices of eggplant so that they form a layer over the top of each one. Spoon dressing on top to coat well.

Let stand for at least 1 hour at room temperature.

If you are keeping the salad for more than 3 or 4 hours, cover and refrigerate but allow to return to room temperature before serving.

Tomato and Basil with Pasta

The Italians have a wonderful pasta dish in which a tomato and basil-flavoured sauce is chilled before it is poured over hot pasta. Although it immediately cools down the pasta, it has the effect of releasing an intense flavour and aroma as the heat and cold combine. It is eaten immediately, slightly lukewarm, and is not heated again or the sauce would lose the fresh taste.

A similar idea is used in this salad. The tomato and basil are cold and when added to either a thin spaghetti or a small macaroni, all the flavours become stronger when stirred into the hot pasta. The difference is that it is left to cool and then served either as a first course or a side dish.

It is a summer-to-autumn dish because fresh basil and sun-ripened tomatoes are necessary and is especially good with scallopini or schnitzel.

Serves 6
250 g (8 oz) fine spaghetti,
  macaroni or shell pasta
1 tablespoon finely
  chopped shallots (or
  spring onions)
1 clove garlic, crushed
250 g (8 oz) ripe tomatoes,
  peeled
$\frac{1}{4}$ cup fresh basil leaves
2 tablespoons finely
  chopped pimento-stuffed
  olives

salt and pepper
$\frac{1}{3}$ cup ($2\frac{1}{2}$ fl oz) olive oil
1 tablespoon lemon juice

Note: If using a shell pasta do not buy the dried commercial variety as it is too heavy for this dish. Only use if you can obtain the fresh, home-made pasta, otherwise spaghetti or small macaroni are the best choice.

Cook the spaghetti or macaroni in a saucepan of rapidly boiling water which has been generously seasoned with salt.

While it is cooking prepare the sauce so that it can be added while the pasta is still warm.

Mix together the shallots and garlic.

Cut the tomatoes into tiny dice. As you do this press out some of the seeds and discard them. It doesn't matter particularly if a little of the juice and seeds are in the mixture, but too much will make the sauce watery.

Add the basil, olives, salt and pepper.

When the pasta is cooked, drain well and leave a moment to make sure no water remains.

Place into a large bowl, add the oil, lemon juice and the tomato mixture and mix well to coat the pasta evenly. Taste, and if not spicy enough add a little extra pepper or salt as needed. The basil will darken as it stands but this will not detract from the flavour.

Leave to cool, but don't refrigerate.

Serve within 4 to 5 hours of making the salad. Before you take it to the table, stir the pasta so that any liquid which has accumulated in the bottom of the bowl is mixed through.

Celeriac salad with Mustard dressing

A rather unattractive looking vegetable, brown with a knobby convoluted exterior, the appearance of celeriac, or celery root as it is often known, belies its delicate flavour. It is used raw in salads or cooked in many ways. It can be grated, sliced, diced and sometimes mashed in a similar fashion to potato.

You need to be careful after peeling celeriac, to use it instantly, or to place it into water which has a little lemon juice or vinegar added since it very quickly turns an unslightly greyish brown. This doesn't change the flavour but it spoils the appearance.

As a salad it is most successful as a first course and can form part of an hors d'oeuvres platter or it can be served mounded in a small bowl with bread and butter. It is also good served with ham. Although the celeriac in this dish is not rich, the dressing is, so you don't need to serve a large portion.

Serve 4
500 g (1 lb) celeriac
1 tablespoon French or
  Dijon mustard
1 teaspoon dry English
  mustard
3 tablespoons olive oil
1 tablespoon white wine
  vinegar
2 tablespoons thick cream
2 tablespoons mayonnaise

Trim the celeriac and peel it. Cut into quarters, sixths or eighths, depending on the size of the root, and then into very thin slices. Place into a pan and cover with cold water. Season with salt and cook for 3 minutes or until just slightly softened. Drain and immediately refresh under cold water.

Mix the mustards, oil and vinegar and whisk until thick. Add the cream and mayonnaise and stir into the celeriac slices. Cover and chill if not using immediately, but remove it from the refrigerator a short time before using or the dressing will become too thick.

Caesar salad

Although several chefs and restaurants claim that the original Caesar Salad was their invention, the best-known story is the one attributing it to Caesar Cardini, who owned a restaurant in Mexico. Catering for a crowd who had stayed late, he mixed a salad using mainly what he had left in the kitchen—some lettuce, cheese, eggs and bread—and created this salad, which has remained popular for almost sixty years.

It is not a salad that is eaten as an accompaniment. It is quite rich and makes a great first course or light lunch.

Like many simple things, it must be done well to be right. You should use the young leaves of cos lettuce; the croûtons need to be really fresh and crisply cooked in good olive oil; the cheese should be freshly grated Parmesan.

The ceremony that goes with the presentation of a Caesar Salad is almost as good as the taste—the big bowl of lettuce, which is turned over until it is shiny with oil, and then the remaining ingredients added one by one. You can perform the ceremony at the table if you wish, but even if you just have the salad ready and add the top garnishing, then toss it, it will still look impressive.

Although you cannot prepare it beforehand, if you have all the ingredients ready, it will take only a few minutes to assemble.

Serves 6 as a first course, 4 for
a light lunch
**2 small heads cos (romaine)
   lettuce**
1 clove garlic
3 tablespoons olive oil
**$\frac{3}{4}$ cup neatly diced white
   bread (crusts removed)**
**an additional 5 tablespoons
   olive oil**
2 tablespoons lemon juice
finely ground pepper
2 eggs
45 g (1$\frac{1}{2}$ oz) anchovy fillets
**2 tablespoons freshly grated
   Parmesan cheese**

Discard the outside heavy green leaves of the lettuce and remove the smaller leaves for the salad. Allow about 5 to 6 per person, but this depends on the size of the leaves.

Heat the garlic and oil very gently in a frying pan. Add the bread and cook, turning until the croûtons are crisp and golden. Drain on kitchen paper. Discard the garlic clove.

Make up the dressing for the salad by mixing the additional olive oil with the lemon juice and pepper.

Boil the eggs for exactly 1 minute.

Cut the anchovy fillets into small pieces.

Place the lettuce into a bowl. If the leaves are very large you can carefully tear them across so they are a little more manageable for eating.

Toss with the dressing so that every leaf is coated and shining. Break the eggs into the salad then mix again; it will make the dressing quite creamy.

Scatter the croûtons on top, add the anchovy fillets and Parmesan cheese and toss again before serving.

Caesar salad (page 36)

Lobster and Avocado salad

An expensive, luxury first course which is exquisite in flavour and, with little effort, can be presented so that it resembles a beautiful still life painting.

Although the pimento and tomato dressing has a fairly assertive flavour, the lobster has sufficient flavour of its own to combine well with it.

This is a rich dish, both lobster and avocado being very satisfying, so follow with something light.

By adding a little extra lobster you could serve this as a main course at lunch.

Serves 4
**1 lobster, weighing 1–1.25
kg (2–2½ lb)
1 avocado
lemon juice
8 small mignonette lettuce
leaves**

Dressing:
**375 g (12 oz) ripe tomatoes,
peeled
1 tablespoon peanut oil
salt and pepper
1 teaspoon sugar
1 × 240 g (7½ oz) tin
pimento
½ cup (4 fl oz) mayonnaise**

To make the dressing, cut the tomatoes into small pieces, discarding some of the juice and seeds.

Place into a saucepan with the peanut oil, salt, pepper and sugar. Cook over a medium heat, uncovered, until the tomato has thickened. The cooking time will depend on how much juice is in the ripe tomatoes. It needs to cook down to a thick paste or the dressing will be too thin.

Place the tomato paste into a food processor. Drain the tinned pimento well, chop the pieces roughly and add to the tomato. Process until puréed.

Cool thoroughly and when slightly chilled mix in the mayonnaise and taste for seasoning. Set aside until required.

For this dish the lobster tail should be left intact because the meat is cut into medallions, so don't cut the lobster in half down the centre.

Using a knife, slice around the section between the tail and the body to loosen the flesh and then remove the tail completely.

With a pair of small sharp scissors or a knife, cut away the underneath shell of the tail along both edges. Once this is removed the flesh can be slipped out in one long piece.

Cut the tail meat into medallions, at the same time removing the little intestinal vein. Set aside 8 of the nicest medallions. Dice the rest and place into a bowl.

Reserve 8 legs from the lobster and crack the remaining legs to remove the flesh.

Cut the body of the lobster and remove as much of the meat as possible. Combine with the meat from the legs and the diced medallions.

Mix the diced lobster, with sufficient pimento and tomato dressing to make it quite moist.

Cover the reserved medallions and the diced lobster meat tightly and chill them.

Assemble the salad about 30 minutes before serving.

Cut the avocado in half and remove the stone. Peel the avocado and cut it into long thin slices, allowing about 4 to 5 slices from each quarter. Squeeze a little lemon juice over them and arrange the slices in a fan shape on one side of individual plates.

Place two overlapping mignonette lettuce leaves at the top of each plate and place some lobster meat into these. Spoon a little dressing along the side opposite the avocado and arrange the medallions of lobster on top of the dressing, decorating with the legs.

You may have some dressing left over; this can either be served at the table or kept refrigerated. It will keep well for about 5 days.

Crab salad

Crab is moist and sweet and one of the most succulent and mouth-watering of all shellfish. But in proportion to size and shell structure there is not a great deal of flesh on a crab.

There is something a little intimidating about being confronted by a live crab. They have hard shells and even when the front claws are tied, appear ferocious.

You can buy them ready cooked for the salad, which makes it easier, but if you have to prepare the crab yourself it is really quite simple.

First drown the crab in fresh water, then bring a pot of generously salted water to the boil, immerse the crab and simmer gently for about 25 to 30 minutes for a crab weighing 1.5 kg (3 lb). Leave to cool completely before shelling the crab for the salad.

The mayonnaise dressing on the crab is equally successful as a sauce for lobster.

Serves 4 as a first course, 2 for a main course
**1 cooked crab weighing
approximately 1.5 kg
(3 lb)**

Mayonnaise:
**1 tablespoon vegetable oil
1 teaspoon white vinegar
1 teaspoon French mustard
¼ cup (2 fl oz) oil
mayonnaise
½ teaspoon Worcestershire
sauce
1 tablespoon tomato sauce
(ketchup)
1 tablespoon grated
horseradish or relish
salt and pepper
2 tablespoons lightly
whipped cream
1 small lettuce
1 hard-boiled egg**

To extract all the meat from the crab, turn it on its back and remove the legs and claws, twisting them at the joints where they are attached to the body. Crack and remove the flesh. Hold firmly, twist off the underside shell by gripping where the legs were removed and pull apart the carapace and underneath section.

Pull away and discard the feathery gills and if you like the 'mustard' keep and mix into the mayonnaise. Carefully remove all the meat, discarding the mass of semi-transparent bone.

Wash the shell to use in the salad.

Mix all the mayonnaise ingredients together and gently stir through the crab flesh. Chill well. It can be left refrigerated for about 6 hours if you wish.

To serve, fill the mixture into the shell and place the shell on some lettuce leaves.

Cut the hard-boiled egg in half. Sieve the yolk and cut the white into tiny strips. Scatter the white around the edge and the yolk in the centre.

Serve at the table, spooning each portion onto lettuce.

Scallop and Mango salad

If you like the combination of fruit and seafood this is a very good choice. While it does not have a dressing, the mango could have a little lemon juice squeezed over the top, although the scallops have sufficient flavour from the cooking liquid. I prefer not even to dress the lettuce with any oil or vinegar because I find that it detracts from the fresh taste of the salad.

Serves 4

500 g (1 lb) scallops	**1 garlic clove**
$\frac{1}{2}$ cup (4 fl oz) water	**1 tablespoon honey**
$\frac{1}{2}$ cup (4 fl oz) white wine	**salt**
1 thick strip fresh green	**some lemon juice**
ginger	**8 spring onions (scallions)**
1 tablespoon soy sauce	**2 small or 1 large mango**
	1 mignonette lettuce

Trim the scallops of any tiny black sections on the side. Heat the water, wine, ginger, soy sauce, garlic clove, honey and salt and leave the mixture to simmer gently for about 5 minutes.

Add the scallops, cook only 1 minute, remove the pan from the heat and let the scallops stand in the hot liquid for another 1 or 2 minutes, depending on their size.

Remove the scallops from the liquid, using a slotted spoon. Put the liquid aside and place the scallops on a plate. Place another plate on top to keep them moist.

Cut the spring onions into large chunky pieces and add to the liquid. Boil until the liquid has reduced to about $\frac{1}{3}$ cup ($2\frac{1}{2}$ fl oz) and the spring onions are soft. Discard garlic and ginger. Mix the liquid into the scallops.

Place some mignonette lettuce on individual plates. Peel the mango and cut thin slices from it. Overlap these on the lettuce. Squeeze a little lemon juice on top. Place the scallops in the centre of the mango. Serve within 15 minutes, while the lettuce is still crisp.

Crab and Prawn salad in Orange Shells

Freshly cooked crab used in a salad is so sweet that it really needs little ornamentation. However, fresh crabs are not always easy to obtain. In this salad, tinned crab is used, but since it doesn't have quite the same flavour it is improved by some 'gilding of the lily'.

Crab meat is light and flaky and the addition of firmer pieces of prawn adds more texture.

Served in an orange shell it looks attractive as a first course and the fruit with the seafood makes the dish light and refreshing.

You can prepare the mixture several hours beforehand and it can be chilled for some time without spoiling the flavour or texture. However, place it in the shells and decorate only about 20 minutes before serving.

Serves 4	Dressing:
2 medium-sized oranges	**3 tablespoons thick cream**
1 × 185 g (12 oz) tin crabmeat	**1 tablespoon orange juice**
	$\frac{1}{4}$ teaspoon Tabasco
125 g (4 oz) shelled cooked prawns	**1 tablespoon mayonnaise**
	2 teaspoons tomato sauce
4 mignonette lettuce leaves	**2 teaspoons lemon juice**
1 additional orange for garnishing	
few long strands of chives	

Cut the oranges in half and remove all the flesh, leaving the shells for serving. You need a little of the juice for the dressing but the remainder of the orange will not be used in this dish.

Remove any membrane from the crab and place the crab meat into a bowl.

Chop the prawns into small pieces and mix with the crab.

To make the dressing, mix all the ingredients together and taste for seasoning. It should be slightly spicy. Chill, covered, if not using immediately. It can be kept for 12 hours. (You will find this makes a generous amount but the crab needs to be very well coated.)

Mix the dressing through the crab and prawn mixture. Cover and chill for 1 hour or longer.

Place 1 lettuce leaf in each orange shell so that one side shows well above the edge. Fill the shells with the crab and prawn salad.

Remove all the skin and pith from the additional orange, leaving only the flesh. Cut out segments from the orange, leaving the membrane behind. You need 8 segments to garnish the dish.

Place 2 segments on each shell, on the opposite side to the lettuce and tucked along the edge, and decorate with a strip of chive.

Springtime Scallops (page 49)

Crab and Prawn salad in Orange Shells (page 39)

Lobster and Avocado salad (page 38)

Scallop and Potato salad

Serve this salad in a cupped lettuce leaf or a small dish and arrange it so that some of the lovely pink coral is on top. If it is a time of the year when the coral is very pale, add a few shreds of peeled tomato to give added interest to the dish, which has a lot of flavour but little colour. This salad does not improve by standing so make it as close to serving time as possible.

Serves 4

**250 g (8 oz) small new
  potatoes**
375 g (12 oz) scallops
$\frac{1}{2}$ **cup (4 fl oz) water**
$\frac{1}{2}$ **cup (4 fl oz) dry white
  wine**
salt and pepper
**parsley sprigs, including
  some stalks**
**1 small white onion, finely
  diced**

Dressing:

$\frac{1}{2}$ **cup (4 fl oz) vegetable oil**
1 tablespoon lemon juice
**1 tablespoon white wine
  vinegar**
1 teaspoon sugar
**2 tablespoons finely
  chopped parsley**
**1 tablespoon finely
  chopped chervil**
**1 teaspoon dry,
  English-style mustard**
**1 tablespoon chopped
  capers**
**2 tablespoons chopped
  sweet-sour cucumbers**
1 hard-boiled egg
salt and pepper

Cook the potatoes, unpeeled, in a pot of salted water until tender. Drain and leave to cool slightly so that they can be easily handled.

Trim and clean the scallops, reserving the coral.

Heat the water, wine, salt and pepper with some parsley sprigs added. Add the scallops and simmer for 1 minute.

Remove from the heat and drain them. Place the scallops on a plate and press another plate lightly on top until the scallops cool a little.

If they are very large, cut the scallops in half or slice them; if they are small, leave them whole.

Slice the potatoes and mix them gently with the scallops and dressing.

To make the dressing, mix the oil with the lemon juice, vinegar, sugar, parsley, chervil, mustard, capers and cucumbers. Chop the hard-boiled egg roughly and mix through; season with salt and pepper.

This dressing can be made up to 12 hours beforehand. Refrigerate, but remove some time before using because it will become very thick when chilled.

Season the salad well and keep covered but not refrigerated, if possible, because once it is chilled it loses some of its fresh flavour.

Cucumber and Prawn salad

Only a few ingredients are required to make this extraordinarily good salad which has lemon juice and chopped fresh coriander with freshly cooked green (raw) prawns.

The dish is not so successful if you use cooked prawns. Instead of the shellfish being sweet and juicy they become dry and don't absorb any of the flavourings.

I like to use the raw prawns in the shell and peel these, leaving some of the tail on mainly for appearance. If you don't want to go to the bother of peeling them, use the ready-shelled ones.

The prawns should not be cooked until the last moment but the plates can be made ready, with the lettuce arranged to form a base, and the ingredients all prepared in advance. It is then only a matter of spending a few minutes to cook the shellfish when you are ready to serve the course.

Serves 4

**1 medium-sized cucumber,
  about 375 g (12 oz)**
salt
1 teaspoon sugar
1 tablespoon lemon juice
24 green prawns
lettuce leaves

1 small dried chilli
black pepper and salt
**approx. 1 tablespoon extra
  lemon juice**
**1 tablespoon finely
  chopped fresh coriander
  (Chinese parsley)**

Peel the cucumber, score the sides with a fork and cut into wafer-thin slices. Place these in a basin and add salt, sugar and 1 tablespoon of lemon juice. Leave them to stand for at least 30 minutes.

Shell and devein the prawns, leaving the tail end of the shell intact.

Arrange the lettuce leaves on individual plates.

Squeeze the moisture from the cucumber and arrange the slices over the lettuce.

Heat the oil in a frying pan and add the chilli. Add the prawns and lightly toss them over fairly high heat until they have changed colour on the outside and are just barely cooked through. They take only a few minutes and must not be overcooked or they will toughen.

Remove the chilli from the oil. Season the prawns with salt and pepper. Add the lemon juice and the coriander and remove the pan from the heat instantly.

Shake or stir gently to coat the prawns and immediately spoon the hot prawns, together with the pan juices, over the cucumber.

Avocado and Prawn mould

This is a very bright and colourful dish because of the natural green of the avocado combined with a seafood mixture. It has layers of avocado on the top and base and is set with gelatine. It does not discolour, provided lemon is used in the mixture, but has limited keeping qualities. It is perfect for about 12 hours, then the green changes colour, so make it on the morning of a dinner party, or the evening before a lunch.

Because both the avocado and prawn are cold and uncooked, once the gelatine is added they will set very rapidly, so when you place the first layer of avocado in the refrigerator, be sure to keep the remainder at room temperature. If by any chance it does begin to set, stand the bowl in a dish of warm water.

You can use either a log-shaped mould, or a square one if you want to serve slices, or a round container can be used, in which case cut it in wedges. Don't use metal; a china soufflé dish, a terrine container or a china or glass bowl would be ideal.

It is rich, so offer only small portions and accompany simply with brown bread and butter.

If you serve this as a main lunch dish, a crisp fresh salad with celery or endive (witlof) is best.

Serves 8 as a first course or 4 for a main course

Avocado Layer:
- **2 avocados, about 450 g (1 lb) altogether**
- **2 tablespoons lemon juice**
- **1 teaspoon Worcestershire sauce**
- **2 tablespoons mayonnaise**
- **salt and pepper**
- **3 teaspoons gelatine**
- **2 tablespoons water**
- **4 half prawns, cut lengthwise**

Prawn Filling:
- **500 g (1 lb) cooked prawns, in their shells**
- **2 hard-boiled eggs**
- **1 teaspoon mild curry powder**
- **2 tablespoons mayonnaise**
- **2 teaspoons lemon juice**
- **2 tablespoons tomato sauce (ketchup)**
- **$\frac{1}{2}$ cup (4 fl oz) cream, lightly whipped**
- **3 teaspoons gelatine**
- **2 tablespoons water**

Cut the avocados in half and twist to remove from the stone. Peel them and cut away four thin slices lengthwise. These are to be used for decoration. Brush with some lemon juice immediately and cover tightly to prevent discolouration while preparing the remainder of the mixture.

Purée the avocados in a food processor, or mash them. If you do mash them, they will not have the same fine texture but will still be quite satisfactory.

Add the lemon juice, Worcestershire sauce, mayonnaise and salt and pepper. Taste it; it should be fresh-tasting and well seasoned.

In a cup, mix the gelatine with the water and stir it all in. Stand the cup in a bowl of warm water and leave until the gelatine is clear. Mix into the avocado. (If the avocado mixture is cold, it is safer to add a little of it to the gelatine first, to prevent it setting too quickly.)

Use a mould which holds about 4 cups (1 litre); if you are not confident about turning out the mould, line it with some lightly-oiled paper.

Arrange the four slices of avocado in the base of the mould, forming a star shape graduating from the centre. Arrange the 4 slices of prawn between them.

Spoon half the avocado mixture carefully over the decoration so as not to disturb it. Refrigerate this section immediately so that it will set quickly and leave the other half of the mixture at room temperature.

Peel the prawns and cut them into small pieces.

Cut the eggs into pieces much the same size as the prawns.

Mix the curry powder with the mayonnaise, lemon juice, tomato sauce and cream. Stir it through the prawns and eggs.

Mix the gelatine and water together, stirring well, then stand it in warm water until dissolved.

When clear, mix some of the mayonnaise mixture into the gelatine, then return it to the bowl, stirring well.

Pour this carefully over the avocado layer, which should be firm by now.

Refrigerate again. As a rule, the seafood mixture will begin to set in about 20 minutes. As soon as this happens, add the remainder of the avocado, cover and chill again.

To serve, dip the mould in warm water and turn out onto a plate. It keeps better in the container, so leave it until close to dinner time. Either slice or serve in wedges.

Salmon Mousse

Among cold fish dishes, it is hard to better a light, salmon mousse as a first course. It has an advantage in that it can be completely prepared well beforehand and presents beautifully, either in a fish mould or a round shape.

No mayonnaise needs to be served with this as the dish has sufficient flavour of its own.

If you wish to serve an accompaniment, a cucumber salad is the best choice.

Serves 8
- **2 × 220 g (7$\frac{1}{2}$ oz) tins red salmon**
- **1 tablespoon sugar**
- **1 teaspoon dry, English-style mustard**
- **$\frac{1}{2}$ cup (4 fl oz) white wine vinegar**
- **1 tablespoon gelatine**
- **$\frac{1}{4}$ cup (2 fl oz) water**
- **1 tablespoon horseradish relish**
- **1 tablespoon mayonnaise**
- **1 cup finely diced celery**
- **2 teaspoons finely chopped, drained capers**
- **2 tablespoons finely chopped spring onions (scallions)**
- **2 tablespoons sweet-sour cucumber**
- **$\frac{1}{2}$ cup (4 fl oz) cream, lightly whipped**

Remove any little pieces of bone from the salmon. Place into a food processor or a blender with the sugar, mustard, and wine vinegar and process until smooth.

Mix the gelatine with the water and stir to include any dry bits. Dissolve in a cup standing in hot water.

Mix together the horseradish, mayonnaise and gelatine and stir this into the salmon.

Add the celery, capers, spring onions and cucumber. Lastly, fold in the cream.

Pour into a lightly oiled mould with a capacity of 4 cups (32 fl oz) and leave to set in the refrigerator. Covered, it keeps perfectly for about 36 hours.

Dip the mould lightly in warm water and then unmould the mousse carefully onto a serving platter.

Salmon Mousse (above)

Bagatelle salad

When the first national non-commercial restaurant guide of Australia was published in 1982, only one restaurant, Bagatelle received the top award of five stars for food, giving the chef the automatic recognition of being the best in the country.

Jean Luc Lundy is a young Frenchman, who trained and worked in some great overseas restaurants before coming to Australia.

His presentation is imaginative and exquisite and he believes that fresh food should be cooked quickly but quite simply.

This salad is served occasionally as a first course at Bagatelle. It was inspired he says by one which he first tasted at the famous three Star restaurant of Roger Vergé, Moulin de Mougins.

The salad uses green prawns which are marinated in lemon juice so they are 'cooked' by the acid. Some of the lemon juice is later mixed with oil to make the dressing. It should be tart but not too sharp, so adjust accordingly when you make it.

Served with tomato, avocado and mushroom, it makes a substantial first course to be followed by a light main dish. Or it could be served for a lunch, accompanied by some crusty bread.

Serves 6

24 green king prawns (jumbo shrimp)	(chinese parsley), finely chopped
1½ cups (12 fl oz) lemon juice	¼ teaspoon finely chopped red chilli
2 tablespoons finely chopped shallots or spring onions	pinch salt
	¾ cup (6 fl oz) olive oil
1 clove garlic, crushed	3 small ripe avocadoes
2 tablespoons coriander	3 medium sized tomatoes, peeled
	3 large white mushrooms

Peel the prawns and devein them.

Cut into half lengthwise.

Mix together the lemon juice, shallots, garlic, coriander, chilli and salt. Add the prawns and stir carefully to coat them well. Leave to stand for at least 2 hours, covered and refrigerated. They will become opaque.

When ready to serve, cut the avocadoes in half, twist to remove from the stone and carefully peel them. Cut into slices. Cut the tomatoes into slices. Wipe the mushroom caps, cut the stalks level and slice thinly. Drain the prawns.

Measure ¼ cup of the lemon juice mixture and whisk into the olive oil until thick.

Arrange the avocadoes at the top of a plate. Arrange the tomato slices on one side of the plate and the mushroom on the other side.

Place the prawns in the centre and spoon the dressing over the salad.

Once prepared, serve immediately.

Tomatoes filled with Cucumber and Salmon

A very simple dish, always popular because of its fresh taste and attractive presentation.

It is essential to have very ripe and fresh tomatoes; early season or winter tomatoes will be lacking in flavour.

I have suggested salmon, but tuna or chopped prawns could be substituted for an equally good result. If you are using prawns, you may like to try adding coriander (Chinese parsley) instead of the dill.

It is best to fill the tomatoes shortly before they are to be served, although the filling can be made well in advance.

This is a good first course or even a light lunch and if you are serving it as a main dish, a green salad or one of the rice dishes would go well with it.

Serves 4	Dressing:
4 medium-sized ripe tomatoes	⅓ cup (2½ fl oz) mayonnaise
salt and pepper	2 tablespoons yogurt
½ teaspoon sugar	1 tablespoon finely chopped fresh dill
½ cucumber	1 teaspoon hot dry English mustard
1 × 185 g (6 oz) tin red salmon	salt and pepper

Put the tomatoes into boiling water and leave just long enough to loosen the skins, then peel them. Be careful not to leave them in the water too long or they will become soft and will be difficult to handle. Chill the tomatoes slightly. .

Place the tomatoes on a board, using the flatter stalk end as the base, so they will balance more easily. Cut a third off the tops of the tomatoes, to use as a lid. Scoop out the seeds and the insides to form a hollow case. Season with salt, pepper and a little sugar and chill again.

Peel the cucumber and cut it lengthwise. Remove the seeds and cut the cucumber into fine, small julienne strips. Season with salt and a little sugar and let it stand for at least 30 minutes. Drain well and squeeze dry.

Drain the salmon well, remove the bones and mash the flesh lightly. Mix with the cucumber and the dressing.

To make the dressing, mix the mayonnaise and yogurt and add the dill. Mix in the mustard and season well.

Shortly before serving time, drain the chilled tomatoes and fill them with the mixture, heaping it high. Place the top of the tomato back on, tilting it on the side.

Serve cold, but not too chilled or it will lack flavour.

Marinated Fish and Mango salad (page 49)

Spinach and Bacon salad (page 128)

Sliced Avocado with Walnut dressing (page 28)

Asparagus and Prawn salad (page 30)

Vegetable salad with Basil and fresh Tomato sauce (page 116)

Vistafjord Herring salad

M.S. Vistafjord is one of the luxury cruise ships of the Norwegian America Line. The relaxed tempo of ship life gradually settles into a routine where the major decisions of the day revolve around what to choose or not to choose from the menus.

Although international in character, some Scandinavian specialties are listed on the menu. Each day for lunch a variety of the herring salads, traditional as a first course in Sweden is presented. Plain herrings, marinated herrings, herrings in sour cream, herrings with mushrooms, or sometimes this particular rather spiced herring salad, are served.

This salad can be kept for 24 hours, or even longer, but as it stands the herring flavour spreads throughout and becomes stronger.

You can serve it with a pumpernickel or rye bread as a first course but it also is good as a main dish for a light lunch.

Serves 8

500 g (1 lb) small potatoes, preferably new ones
250 g (8 oz) beetroot (beets)
250 g (8 oz) Granny Smith apples
250 g (8 oz) Matjes herring fillets
1 large white onion, finely diced

Dressing:
1 tablespoon sugar
1 tablespoon dry, hot English-style mustard
1 tablespoon white wine vinegar

Topping:
½ cup (4 fl oz) cream, lightly whipped
2 hard-boiled eggs, finely chopped

Place the potatoes into salted water and cook in their skins until tender. Drain and leave to cool. Peel them and cut into small dice.

Cook the beetroot in salted water until tender and when cool remove the skins. Dice the beetroot about the same size as the potato.

Peel and core the apples. Dice and mix with the potato and beetroot.

Cut the herrings into small pieces, or into strips, and mix through with the onion. Season well.

Mix together the dressing ingredients. Stir into the salad mixture and leave to stand, covered, in the refrigerator for several hours. (Although there may not appear to be sufficient dressing to flavour the dish, the herrings themselves impart moisture and flavour to the ingredients.)

Arrange the salad in a mound on a platter. Smooth the top and spread with the cream. Scatter the chopped egg over the cream. The cream will become pink if the dish is allowed to stand for over an hour so do this part of the dish close to serving time, for the sake of appearance rather than the fact that it will affect the taste.

Autumn salad

The name of this salad comes from the collection of ingredients, which are all at their best and most reasonably priced as summer days lengthen into the cooler autumn months. Tomatoes, green peppers and cucumber are combined with potato to make a base which is formed into a cake shape.

It is topped with what could probably be referred to as the poor relation to most fish—sardines. In their tinned state they rarely seem to be considered worthy of creating any special dishes, but in this salad their slightly oily, rich taste blends perfectly with the vegetables.

You can make the base well in advance and although it may become very moist and liquid may accumulate, this won't impair the flavour. Just drain away the excess liquid before placing into the tin to form the bed for the sardines which, arranged on top, form a pattern like the spokes of a wheel. Sardines are usually beautifully, but firmly, packed in their tins, so take care when removing them that they remain intact and retain their shape.

Serves 6

1 small cucumber (about 250 g) (8 oz)
salt
sugar
2 medium-sized ripe tomatoes, peeled
250 g (8 oz) small potatoes
1 small green pepper (capsicum), finely diced
1 medium-sized white onion, finely diced
12 green olives, pimento stuffed
2 tins sardines (220g (7 oz) altogether)
2 hard-boiled eggs

Dressing:
¼ cup (2 fl oz) mayonnaise
1 tablespoon cream
2 tablespoons vegetable oil
1 tablespoon lemon juice
2 teaspoons fresh dill, finely chopped
salt and pepper

Peel the cucumber, cut in half lengthwise and then slice wafer thin. Sprinkle with a little salt and sugar and leave to stand for about 30 minutes.

Drain and squeeze out the liquid.

Cut the tomatoes into tiny pieces, draining away some of the juice and seeds.

Cook the potatoes, in their jackets, in salted water. Drain, and when cool enough to handle, remove the skins. Dice them into small pieces.

Chop the olives roughly and mix everything together except the sardines and the eggs.

Mix together the dressing ingredients, add to the mixture and stir well. Cover and refrigerate.

Lightly oil a cake tin, about 23 cm (9 inches) in diameter. Place the salad in the tin, press down firmly but don't squash the mixture.

Invert the tin and turn out the mixture onto a round platter. If it doesn't come out perfectly you can smooth over the top.

Carefully remove the sardines from the tin and arrange them in the centre of the salad so the tails are towards the centre and the heads at the edge.

Chop the eggs in half and push the yolks through a fine sieve. Chop the whites very finely.

Place the sieved yolks in the centre and the whites in a layer around the edge.

Once the salad is assembled, serve within an hour. If it is allowed to stand excess moisture will accumulate on the plate. If this happens, tilt the plate gently and drain away the excess liquid.

Marinated Fish and Mango salad

This type of fish salad originated in tropical islands where the waters teem with an abundance of fresh fish.

Sliced into small pieces and coated with sharp lime juice, the acid in the fruit will 'cook' the fish.

There are now many versions of the original simple idea; coconut milk can be added; some onions; it can be spiced with a little chilli or mixed with tomato.

The most important thing is to have very fresh fish and one with a fine rather than a coarse texture. To make it easier to eat, all the bones should be removed before the fish is mixed with the juice.

As limes are not easy to obtain, I usually use lemon juice and although it does not have quite the same flavour, the dish works just as well.

The colour of the fish changes from translucent to opaque as the acid soaks in. The flavour is not as 'fishy' as cooked fish, but is much lighter and fresher.

You can decorate this dish in several different ways, for instance, serve it in a shell at the table or, as in this recipe, in lettuce with mango slices.

Serves 6	
500 g (1 lb) fine-textured fish fillets	**$\frac{1}{2}$ cup (4 fl oz) coconut milk**
5 tablespoons lemon juice	**salt**
1 white or spanish onion, finely diced	**6 lettuce leaves**
1 teaspoon fresh chilli, finely chopped	**1 large or 2 small mangoes**

Remove any skin from the fish and check carefully to see that no bones have been left.

Cut the fish into fine strips or slices and then cut these across so they measure about 2.5 × 4 cm (1 × 1$\frac{1}{2}$ inches).

Place into a shallow china or earthenware dish, and add the lemon juice. Turn the fish so that it is well covered and leave in the refrigerator for about 12 hours or until the fish has become opaque instead of translucent.

Drain away the liquid around the fish. Place into a bowl and mix in the onion, chilli and coconut milk and season with salt. Chill well; it can be left another 8 hours without spoiling.

When ready to serve, arrange the lettuce on a plate and spoon the salad onto one side of the lettuce, forming a mound.

Skin the mango and cut away some thin slices. Arrange the slices in a fan shape on the other side of the plate.

Springtime Scallops

One of our most basic vegetables, carrots were once considered exotic and rare, the light feathery leaves used along with the root as a decoration for hats, suits or as an indoor plant.

Tasting the flavour and sweetness of young spring carrots only emphasises how bland this product is in its frozen state.

Young carrots make an exquisite sauce which is wonderful with fish, or in this case scallops. It contains a little orange juice to freshen the dish; if the oranges are very sweet you can add a few teaspoons of lemon juice after tasting the sauce. It should not be acid in flavour however, rather more light and fresh.

Serves 4	
500 g (1 lb) scallops	**100 g (3$\frac{1}{2}$ oz) finely diced carrot**
1 cup (8 fl oz) white wine	**1 teaspoon sugar**
1 cup (8 fl oz) water	**pepper**
few sprigs parsley	**butter or mignonette lettuce**
1 slice onion	**2 oranges to garnish**
salt and pepper	
$\frac{1}{4}$ cup (2 fl oz) orange juice	

Clean the scallops, removing any dark section on the side. If you remove the coral, reserve it for use in the salad.

Heat the wine and water together with the parsley and onion. Season very lightly. When it comes to the boil add the scallops. Simmer them for about 2 minutes if large, 1 minute if tiny, or until just barely cooked. Be very careful not to overcook the scallops or they will become too firm and shrink. Remove to a plate, using a slotted spoon. Place another plate on top to keep them moist.

Remove the onion and parsley from the liquid and boil the liquid until it is reduced to about $\frac{1}{4}$ cup (2 fl oz).

Add the orange juice, carrot and sugar. Cover and cook until the carrot is quite soft. Place the mixture into a blender and blend until it is puréed.

You could use a food processor but since this is not a large amount of sauce, it may not become quite smooth enough. The mixture should be just thick enough to lightly coat a spoon. If it is not thick enough, boil again for a few minutes, uncovered, to reduce it. Leave to cool and then add it to the scallops. Season if necessary.

Cover and chill if keeping for more than a couple of hours, but since this salad is nicest if not served too cold, remove from the refrigerator a short time before serving.

Place 4 butter or mignonette lettuce leaves on a plate, with the stalk ends towards the centre.

At the last moment, stir the scallops to thoroughly coat them with the sauce. Place in a mound in the centre of the lettuce-lined plate.

Remove the skin and white pith from the oranges. Cut into segments. (This could be done beforehand and the segments chilled.) Arrange the orange segments between the lettuce leaves.

Tomato and Basil with Pasta (page 35)

Salad St Tropez (page 25)

Potato salad with Smoked Salmon and Caviar (page 134)

Squid salad

Although popular in so many countries throughout the world, until recently squid was only used as fishing bait in Australia and was not considered worthy of the dinner table.

It makes an interesting salad and is very light in flavour, making it an unusual yet ideal first course.

Great care must be taken not to overcook squid because if it is even slightly overcooked it will become rubbery and tough.

The cooking time will depend on the size of the squid. If possible, I buy the small, rather than the large ones. Ideally, I like them about 50 g (1½ oz), but if you can't obtain these the larger ones, which may weigh up to 200 g (6½ oz), can be used.

If you make a mistake and overcook the squid, you can then simmer them for a long time and they will become tender but with a different texture. To do this, place into a saucepan, add a cup of water, a little lemon juice and some salt, cover and cook over low heat for about 1½ hours.

This particular salad has an Oriental flavour, with the use of the pungent Vietnamese mint. Alternatively, a little fresh coriander could be used instead, but if you don't have a liking for either of these herbs, just use the parsley.

Serves 4

375 g (12 oz) small squid
2 tablespoons oil
½ cup (4 oz) carrot, grated in long shreds
2 tablespoons finely chopped onion
4 Vietnamese mint leaves, finely chopped
1 tablespoon finely chopped parsley
lettuce leaves

Dressing:

2 tablespoons lemon juice
1 tablespoon water
1 tablespoon Vietnamese fish sauce or 2 teaspoons anchovy sauce
3 teaspoons sugar
1 clove crushed garlic
generous pinch cayenne pepper

Squid can be bought already cleaned, but if it is not, don't be daunted by the idea of cleaning it, for it is quite simple.

Cut the tentacles from the head and retain these for use in the salad. Pull the head from the body and discard the head and the entrails. Thoroughly wash the body of the squid. Peel away the fine brown skin and pull out the transparent bone. Cut the squid into small rings. If the tentacles are large, remove the skin, but if they are small there is no need.

In a frying pan, heat the oil. Add the squid and toss until the flesh becomes milky white. It will set into small rings as it begins to cook. Allow only about 20 seconds for baby squid, 30 seconds to a minute for larger pieces. The moment it is cooked, remove from the heat.

Drain on paper towels and place in a bowl. Mix with the carrot, onion, mint leaves, parsley and the dressing.

To make the dressing, mix together the lemon juice, water, fish sauce, sugar, garlic and pepper. Don't add salt as the Vietnamese fish sauce or anchovy sauce will provide plenty. There should be sufficient cayenne to make the dressing spicy, but don't add too much or it will drown the flavour of the squid.

Allow to marinate for at least 1 hour. Although the squid will become slightly firmer when refrigerated it can be kept for 24 hours, covered, if you wish.

To serve, place a little of the squid in the centre of cup-shaped lettuce leaves.

Squid salad (opposite)

Brain salad Julianne

Most people fall into one of two distinct groups—those who love offal and those who neither like preparing it nor eating it.

If you enjoy eating brains, this is one of the most exquisite salads. The brains have a delicate and subtle taste, a creamy texture, firm and yet melting on the palate, with a slight crunch of walnuts on top to add texture.

Obviously it is important to buy really good, fresh brains. They should be quite firm in appearance, the surface moist and the form cleanly defined.

Even when cooking brains with a coating such as breadcrumbs, it is necessary to carefully remove all the membrane and even more essential in a salad.

Serves 4

2 sets lamb's brains
1 tablespoon white wine
  vinegar
1 teaspoon salt
sprig of thyme
sprig of parsley

Salad:
100 g ($3\frac{1}{2}$ oz) small
  mushrooms
salt and pepper
1 tablespoon lemon juice
$\frac{1}{2}$ cucumber
salt
1 teaspoon sugar
1 tablespoon capers
2 tablespoons chopped
  walnuts

Dressing:
$\frac{1}{3}$ cup ($2\frac{1}{2}$ fl oz) mayonnaise
1 tablespoon French
  mustard
$\frac{1}{2}$ teaspoon hot,
  English-style mustard
2 tablespoons cream

Leave the brains to soak in cold water for at least 30 minutes. The vein-threaded surface of the brains must be carefully peeled away. Usually, if the brains are fresh, it will slip free and any little remaining pieces must be peeled as best you can because there should be no membrane remaining at all.

If the brains are bloodstained, place again in cold water to soak, adding a little salt.

Place several cups of cold water into a saucepan, add the vinegar, salt, thyme and parsley. Bring to the boil and simmer for 1 minute. Add the brains and cover the pan. The water should be kept at the barest simmer. Cooking time will depend on the size of the brains but about 10 minutes should be sufficient.

Place the brains into a basin, cover them with the cooking liquid and leave to stand until cool. Refrigerate in the liquid. This can be done several hours before you start to prepare the salad.

To make the salad, cut the mushrooms into thin slices. Remove the stalks if they are tough. Season with salt, pepper and the lemon. Leave to stand for about 30 minutes.

Peel the cucumber and score the sides. Cut into wafer-thin slices. Season with salt and sugar and leave to stand for 30 minutes.

Squeeze the cucumber to remove the moisture.

Mix together all the dressing ingredients. Taste, and if too spicy add a little extra cream.

To assemble the salad, place a small bed of mushrooms on individual plates. Alongside this arrange some overlapping slices of cucumber. Scatter with a few capers.

Cut the brains into thin slices and overlap these on top of the mushrooms.

Place a thin line of dressing along the top of the brains. You should be able to see the slices on either side.

Sprinkle the top of the dressing with the chopped walnuts. Serve the salad within 30 minutes once the dressing has been added or it will lose its fresh taste.

Prosciutto with Melon and Strawberry

Instead of serving just melon with prosciutto, as is customary, the addition of strawberries gives a fresh, slightly sharper flavour.

Use the small berries rather than larger ones and be sure to chill the fruit well.

The fruit is mixed with a dressing made from strawberry vinegar, which can be obtained in many grocery shops or gourmet food shops. If you can't obtain it, you can use a little lemon juice instead.

Have the prosciutto cut wafer-thin, so it is almost transparent. It can vary in flavour and any which is too salty is really not appropriate served with fruit, but is better as a first course with pickled cucumbers and the like.

Serves 4

185 g (6 oz) small
  strawberries
1 small canteloupe or
  melon
12 wafer-thin slices
  prosciutto

Dressing:
1 tablespoon strawberry
  vinegar
3 tablespoons vegetable oil
salt and freshly ground
  black pepper

Hull the strawberries.

Cut the canteloupe or melon in half and remove the seeds. Using a small melon baller, cut out sufficient to allow about 5 to 6 balls per person. Mix with the berries, and chill.

Add the dressing to the fruit about 5 minutes before serving and stir gently. Don't add it earlier than this or it will make the fruit soft.

To make the dressing, mix the vinegar with the oil; whisk it or shake in a jar. Season well. Shake well or whisk before using.

Arrange 3 slices of prosciutto on individual plates, folding them over lightly. Spoon the fruit into the centre.

Smoked Mackerel and Egg salad (page 73)

Main Courses

Sorrel salad with Eggs

Cooked sorrel is used in sauces to give a fresh, sharp taste and it combines especially well with fish or makes an excellent soup.

In this salad it is not cooked but left in fine shreds which are mixed through the salad and with additional sorrel in the dressing, the slight acidity is unusual and refreshing.

If you can't get sorrel, you can squeeze a little extra lemon juice into the dressing instead.

Serves 4
1 cucumber, about 375 g (12 oz)
salt
sugar
$\frac{1}{2}$ cup (4 oz) sultanas (raisins)
1 large apple, cut in small dice
$\frac{1}{4}$ cup (2 oz) peanuts
8 medium-sized sorrel leaves
$\frac{1}{2}$ lettuce
$\frac{1}{3}$ cup (2$\frac{1}{2}$ fl oz) sorrel mayonnaise
6 hard-boiled eggs

Dressing: (see note)
2 egg yolks
1 teaspoon French mustard
3 medium-sized sorrel leaves
1 cup peanut oil
1 tablespoon lemon juice
salt and pepper

Note: You could use a food processor to make the dressing but instead of shreds of sorrel throughout the sauce, it will be a pale green colour. The flavour will be slightly different, and the appearance and texture will be changed.

Peel the cucumber, cut it in half lengthwise and, using a teaspoon, remove the seeds. Cut the cucumber into wafer-thin slices. Place them in a bowl, add a little salt, sprinkle with sugar and allow to stand for about 30 minutes.

Place the sultanas, apple and nuts into a bowl.

If the sorrel has a coarse stalk and vein, remove them. Roll the leaves over firmly, then shred finely.

Cut the lettuce into fine shreds. You need about 2 cups of lettuce.

Mix the lettuce and sorrel together and, using 2 forks, or your hands, lift it to separate the strands.

Mix the lettuce and sorrel into the sultana, nut and apple mixture and add the mayonnaise.

Squeeze the liquid from the cucumber and stir the cucumber into the salad.

Cut the hard-boiled eggs in half, lengthwise.

To make the dressing, place the egg yolks into a dry bowl. (If there is any moisture in the bowl, the dressing may separate.) Add the mustard.

Cut the sorrel leaves into the finest possible shreds, cutting away any tough stalk section. Place the leaves into the bowl and crush them with a wooden spoon. Add the oil gradually, mixing well. Start with a teaspoonful at a time then, as it starts to thicken, you can add it more quickly. When it is thick, add the lemon juice and then, if all the oil has not been added, mix in the remainder to form a creamy, thick mayonnaise. Taste for seasoning. Cover and refrigerate until ready to use.

To assemble, spread the salad on a platter and arrange the eggs around the edge. Coat the top and eggs with the dressing and serve immediately.

Warm Spinach and Egg salad

Although this may sound light, it is substantial enough for a meal, combining fresh green spinach with potatoes, bacon and egg.

The egg is either poached or softly boiled and when broken with a fork, adds creaminess to the dressing that coats the spinach.

Be sure to use spinach, not silver beet and pick out the softest young leaves to form the base of the salad. Although it is a last-minute dish, all the ingredients can be prepared beforehand, the potato diced and left in iced water, bacon and onion chopped and the dressing mixed and kept ready. It then requires only about 15 minutes to cook the various ingredients and serve them warm on the salad.

Serves 4
24 spinach leaves
500 g (1 lb) potatoes
$\frac{1}{3}$ cup (2$\frac{1}{2}$ fl oz) vegetable oil
1 white onion, finely diced
250 g (8 oz) bacon, cut into strips
salt and pepper
4 eggs

Dressing:
6 tablespoons vegetable oil
2 teaspoons French or Dijon mustard
$\frac{1}{2}$ teaspoon dry, English-style mustard
1 teaspoon sugar
1 tablespoon plus 2 teaspoons lemon juice

Wash and dry the spinach well. Carefully remove the stalk and any tough back veins. Place the spinach in the refrigerator to crisp.

Peel the potatoes and cut them into very small dice.

Heat the oil and add the potatoes. Cook, stirring occasionally, until the potatoes are crispy brown on the outside but tender inside. The cooking time will depend on whether the potatoes are new ones or old, but around 12 minutes should be sufficient.

In another pan, cook the onion and bacon together until the bacon is crisp and the onion slightly softened. There should be sufficient bacon fat to cook the onion.

Poach the eggs while the potatoes are cooking, or soft boil them for about 5 minutes and then carefully shell them.

Drain the potatoes and mix them with the onion and bacon in the pan.

Place the spinach on individual plates and pour a little dressing over the top of the leaves.

To make the dressing, mix the oil with the two mustards, add the sugar and whisk in the lemon juice. It should have a thick consistency. (You can make the dressing beforehand, but stir it again before pouring it over the spinach leaves.)

Place the potato mixture in a small mound near the centre of the spinach. Top with the egg and serve immediately.

Salad of Mixed Vegetable with Smoked Salmon and Quail Eggs

This comprises three different salads, although none is very time consuming or difficult to make.

It is a very pretty dish; each salad is arranged separately and around the edge are strips of smoked salmon and quail eggs.

With the increase in quail breeding, the eggs are now quite easy to obtain. Don't use the pickled eggs which you can buy in jars, use fresh hard-boiled ones.

If you can't buy quail eggs use 3 to 4 hard-boiled eggs instead and cut them into wedges.

Other fish could be used instead of smoked salmon, which is very expensive; smoked trout is good as are fresh prawns (jumbo shrimp).

Serves 4

Mushroom Salad:
250 g (8 oz) small, firm button mushrooms
1 tablespoon white wine vinegar
1 tablespoon lemon juice
2 tablespoons finely chopped onion
1 tablespoon finely chopped capers
salt and pepper

Cucumber Salad:
2 medium-sized cucumbers
salt
1 teaspoon sugar
1 tablespoon sour cream
1 teaspoon finely grated lemon rind
1 teaspoon French or Dijon mustard
1 tablespoon finely chopped sweet-sour gherkin
1 teaspoon lemon juice

Alfalfa Salad:
1 cup alfalfa
½ cup finely grated carrot shreds
½ red or green pepper (capsicum), finely shredded

Dressing:
1 tablespoon vegetable oil
2 teaspoons lemon juice

To Finish the Salad:
250 g (8 oz) smoked salmon
16 quail eggs
few sprigs watercress or parsley

Mushroom Salad: Wipe the mushrooms with damp kitchen paper, or wash them. Dry well. Remove the stalks from the mushrooms if they are firm and woody. Cut in half or, if not small mushrooms, into quarters.

Mix with the vinegar, lemon juice, onion and capers and season well. Let it stand for at least 3 hours.

Cucumber Salad: Peel the cucumbers, cut in half, lengthwise. Remove the seeds and cut the cucumber into thick julienne strips. Season with salt and sugar and leave to stand for at least 30 minutes. Drain well, wash if salty and pat dry.

Mix the sour cream, lemon rind, mustard, gherkin and lemon juice, in a basin, and add to the cucumber. Keep chilled.

Alfalfa Salad: Mix the alfalfa, carrot and pepper together. Keep chilled.

Before using, season with salt and pepper and dressing. The salad will become very limp unless you moisten it only at the last moment.

To assemble the salad you will need a large oval or round platter.

Mound the mushrooms in the centre. Drain a little of the liquid if they are wet.

Surround this with the cucumber salad and arrange the alfalfa on the outside.

Roll the smoked salmon into small rolls, arranging them on the alfalfa, and cut the quail eggs in half.

Place the eggs on the salad between the pieces of smoked salmon and decorate with a sprig of watercress or parsley.

Warm Lentil salad with Spiced Sausage

Lentils are usually made into a soup, used as a side dish or made into savoury cakes, but they are quite unusual in a salad. However don't be deterred by this, for they make a spicy, delicious and substantial salad that need not be restricted to warm weather but can make a satisfying meal on a cold winter's night.

It is best to cook the lentils in the late afternoon if you intend using them at night. They should not be cooked too far ahead or they will become dry.

Serves 4
3 tablespoons oil
2 white onions, finely diced
250 g (8 oz) lentils (see note)
500 g (1 lb) tomatoes, peeled and diced
1 teaspoon sugar
2 cups (8 fl oz) water
2 garlic cloves
1 bay leaf
2 teaspoons chopped fresh thyme
salt and pepper
1 tablespoon lemon juice
½ cup finely chopped parsley
375 g (12 oz) Polish or similar sausage
1 white onion
lettuce

Note: Any lentils that are left over can be reheated and served as a vegetable at another meal.

Warm the oil in a saucepan, add the onion and fry gently, stirring occasionally, until slightly softened.

Add the lentils, tomatoes, sugar, water, garlic, bay leaf and thyme and season with a little salt and pepper.

Cook, covered, over very low heat for about an hour or until the lentils are quite soft. Check the pan as they are cooking; if the mixture looks dry, add a little more water.

When the lentils are soft, remove the bay leaf. The garlic cloves will be quite soft and buttery by this stage and can be crushed slightly and mixed through.

Add the lemon juice, check for seasoning and leave the mixture to cool. When cold, add the parsley.

Place the sausage into a pan and cover with water. Cook for about 20 minutes and then peel off the skin. Cut the sausage into thin slices.

While the sausage is cooking, cut the remaining onion in half and then into wafer-thin slices. Place into a bowl of water with some ice and leave them to get very cold and crisp. Drain them well.

Arrange some lettuce around the outside of a platter. Spoon the lentils onto the platter, leaving a space in the centre. Place the warm sausage in the centre and scatter the crisp onion slices over the top.

You can serve this with a little mustard on the side, if you wish, although it is very well-flavoured without it. I like the lettuce plain but if you prefer you can add a little oil and vinegar to the leaves before arranging them on the platter.

Warm Spinach and Egg salad (page 56)

Warm Quail salad (page 104)

Cucumber and Prawn salad (page 42)

Gado Gado

Gado Gado is an Indonesian dish and the custom in that country is to eat it either before or after the main course. It does, however, make an excellent luncheon dish, or could be served as a main course when you don't want to include meat.

The collection of vegetables can be very much a matter of personal choice, and what is in season.

All the various ingredients can be assembled in advance since they are presented cold or at room temperature, and the spicy peanut sauce, called bumbu, can be served either separately at the table or poured over the top just before serving.

The vegetables are cooked, but should retain their crisp texture and bright colour.

In many of the recipes for this dish, peanut butter is used instead of fresh peanuts. Although it is much quicker, the taste of the sauce made with ground peanuts is very much better and the sauce itself is much lighter.

To save time, the sauce can be made several days in advance and then refrigerated.

With some concession to Western palates, this recipe calls for only a small amount of chilli; you can add extra if you wish to make it more authentic.

Serves 4

500 g (1 lb) small potatoes	Sauce: **2 tablespoons peanut oil**
125 g (4 oz) young green beans	**125 g (4 oz) raw peanuts**
4 medium-sized carrots, cut in julienne strips	**1 whole small dried red chilli**
1 cup bean shoots	**2 cloves garlic**
1 small cucumber or ½ a large one	**1 white onion, finely chopped**
2 cups firmly packed shredded Chinese cabbage (see note)	**1 teaspoon shrimp paste (blachan)**
1 white onion, cut in half, then into wafer-thin slices	**1 tablespoon brown sugar**
4 hard-boiled eggs	**2 tablespoons lemon juice**
1 bunch watercress	**1 teaspoon salt**

500 g (1 lb) small potatoes
125 g (4 oz) young green beans
4 medium-sized carrots, cut in julienne strips
1 cup bean shoots
1 small cucumber or ½ a large one
2 cups firmly packed shredded Chinese cabbage (see note)
1 white onion, cut in half, then into wafer-thin slices
4 hard-boiled eggs
1 bunch watercress

Sauce:
2 tablespoons peanut oil
125 g (4 oz) raw peanuts
1 whole small dried red chilli
2 cloves garlic
1 white onion, finely chopped
1 teaspoon shrimp paste (blachan)
1 tablespoon brown sugar
2 tablespoons lemon juice
1 teaspoon salt
1 cup water
¾ cup (6 fl oz) coconut milk

Note: Most recipes call for the cabbage to be blanched for a minute. I prefer it crisper, but you may choose whichever you prefer.

Boil the potatoes, in their jackets, until tender. When they are cool, peel and cut in half, or into thick slices if the potatoes are large.

Cook the beans in salted water until barely tender. Drain and refresh under cold running water.

Boil the carrots for a couple of minutes and refresh in cold water.

Peel the cucumber and cut it into slices.

Pinch and discard the root end from the bean shoots; pour boiling water over them. Drain and refresh with some cold water. This will keep them crisp.

Cut the eggs into quarters.

Discard the heavy stalks from the watercress, leaving only the small sprigs. Chill these until crisp.

Arrange the watercress on a platter and make mounds of the various vegetables on top. Decorate with the wedges of hard-boiled egg.

To make the sauce, heat the oil and cook the peanuts until they are golden in colour. Drain on kitchen paper and then grind them finely in a food processor or a blender. They should be slightly mealy in texture, and oily.

Heat a little fresh oil in the pan and add the chilli. Cook, turning, until it is puffed and crisp. Remove it from the pan. When cooled, chop or crumble it finely, removing most of the seeds.

Cut the garlic into fine slices and add to the same pan, along with the onion. Cook until golden and slightly crisp; don't overcook it. The mixture should be quite fine; if it is not, crush the onion slightly.

Mix in the nuts, brown sugar, lemon, salt, the pieces of chilli and the water.

Place in a small saucepan, return it to the heat and cook gently until lightly thickened.

Add the coconut milk and simmer for a couple of minutes. If the sauce becomes too thick, thin it down with a little water.

The sauce will keep for about 5 days in the refrigerator. If you make it in advance, cook the mixture with the water only and then on the day you are using it, add the coconut milk to thin it down. It should be served cool, or just slightly warm, never chilled.

Coconut milk

1 cup (8 oz) desiccated coconut
1 cup (8 fl oz) boiling water

Place the coconut into a bowl and pour in the boiling water.

Leave to stand until it has partly cooled.

Knead for a minute with your fingers and then press the liquid through a sieve.

You should get about ½–¾ cup of thick coconut milk from this.

Salade Niçoise

Travelling through the area of Provence in France, or on the French Riviera, there is one dish that appears with great regularity on the menus of the smallest cafés as well as the more expensive establishments.

Salade Niçoise, with its robust mixture of flavours and colours, is typical of this famous playground of France.

Like so many famous dishes there are a dozen variations, but the constant ingredients are tuna, anchovies, hard-boiled eggs and the pungent little black olives of the region.

It is the type of salad that needs to be arranged, then served or mixed at the table.

With crusty bread and a light, fresh wine, it is perfect for lunch but also makes a good light first course in the summer.

Serves 4

500 g (1 lb) new potatoes
1 medium-sized white
  onion, finely chopped
salt and pepper
500 g (1 lb) stringless beans
4 hard-boiled eggs
4 ripe tomatoes
1 lettuce
1 × 250 g (8 oz) tin tuna,
  broken into chunky
  pieces
2 tablespoons capers
12 small black olives
3 tablespoons finely
  chopped parsley
45 g (1½ oz) anchovies

Dressing:

1 teaspoon French mustard
1 teaspoon hot, dry
  English-style mustard
1 clove garlic, crushed
1 teaspoon salt
¾ cup (6 fl oz) light olive
  oil
¼ cup (2 fl oz) white wine
  vinegar
black pepper
2 teaspoons finely chopped
  fresh chives
2 teaspoons basil leaves,
  broken into small pieces

First make the dressing.

Mix the mustards with the garlic. Add salt and oil and gradually whisk in the vinegar. Mix in the pepper and herbs. The dressing will separate as it stands, but whisk or shake it in a jar before using.

Cook the potatoes, in their jackets, in salted water until tender. Peel when cool and cut into thick slices.

While still warm, mix the potatoes with the onion, salt and pepper and ⅓ cup (2½ fl oz) dressing. Toss gently and leave to stand for at least 1 hour.

Cut the ends from the beans and either cut in half or leave them whole. Cook in a pan of salted water until tender, but still crisp.

Drain and immediately refresh by running cold water over them until they are cold. They will retain crispness and a bright green colour. Drain well.

Cut the hard-boiled eggs into quarters and the tomatoes into segments.

The ingredients can be made ready and the salad arranged 20 minutes beforehand, but no longer because once the dressing is added the beans etc. lose crispness and some colour.

For this salad, choose a big, wide, rather flat salad bowl, or else a platter which has an indent in the centre.

Mix the lettuce leaves with a spoonful or two of dressing and arrange them around the edge of the bowl or platter. Place a ring of potato salad inside this.

Arrange the quartered eggs and the tomatoes on the inside of the potato.

Mix the beans with a little dressing to moisten. Season well with some additional salt and pepper and place in the centre.

Scatter the tuna, capers and olives over the beans.

Dribble more of the dressing over the top.

Lastly, scatter parsley over the centre and decorate with anchovy fillets.

Once it is served, the impressive appearance is lost, but it should be taken to the table complete. It is automatically tossed as the guests serve themselves.

Curried Fruit in a Pineapple Shell with Chicken

This is a fresh dish which has a light curry sauce and is served in a pineapple shell. The pineapple and apple are indispensable in the recipe, but mango can be used instead of peaches if they are out of season or you could add some extra orange segments. If you want to make this a light lunch, serve some cottage cheese instead of chicken. It is also wonderful with thinly sliced turkey as an accompaniment.

Serves 4

2 medium-sized pineapples
2 eating apples
1 large or 2 small yellow
  peaches
lemon juice
3 oranges
4 chicken breasts
1 cup (8 fl oz) chicken
  stock or water
45 g (1½ oz) macadamia

nuts, cut in slices
2 teaspoons vegetable oil

Sauce:
½ cup fresh pineapple
2 teaspoons mild curry
  powder
1 tablespoon apricot jam
2 tablespoons mayonnaise
2 teaspoons lemon juice
⅓ cup (2½ fl oz) cream

Cut the pineapples in halves lengthwise. Remove the fruit carefully; a grapefruit knife is very good for this, but if the pineapple breaks up a bit it does not matter greatly as the fruit will be diced. Remove the core and cut the fruit into slices. Measure about 2 cups, keep the rest of the fruit for another use. Using a fork, scrape a little of the pulp from the shell. Add a little more of the pineapple, crushing lightly until it measures ½ cup. Keep aside. This is used in the sauce.

Peel, core and cut the apples into chunky dice. Add a little lemon juice to coat. Peel and slice the peaches and pour over a little lemon juice. Remove the skin from the orange, taking away the white bitter pith as well and cut out the segments from the orange so that no membrane remains. Mix all the fruit together, cover and chill.

Remove the skin from the chicken breasts. Bring the chicken stock or seasoned water to the boil in a frying pan and add the chicken. Immediately turn the heat down to very low, the water should not come to the boil again but it should be kept very hot and bubbling occasionally. After about 3 minutes, turn the chicken breasts over. Cook for a further minute, cover the pan and remove it from the heat until the cooking liquid has cooled. Refrigerate the chicken breasts, covered by the liquid, but don't keep them longer than 6 hours or they will become too firm. Heat the nuts with the oil in a pan and cook until a pale golden colour. Drain on paper towels.

To make the sauce, place the crushed pineapple in a frying pan with the curry powder and cook for 1 minute. Remove to a bowl and add the jam. If there are any large pieces of apricot in the jam, cut into small bits with a knife. Mix in the mayonnaise, lemon juice and cream. The sauce can be made hours beforehand and refrigerated.

Mix the sauce with the fruit about 10 minutes before serving and place into the pineapple shells. Sprinkle the nuts on top. Cut the chicken breasts into thin slices and arrange them in a fan on the plate beside the pineapple shell. Season with salt and pepper.

Fruit and Cottage Cheese Platter

During the summer and autumn months there is an array of wonderful fresh fruits available, ranging from the lucious flavour of the tropical varieties to the more fragile berries. These are mostly associated with dessert but in some countries, particularly the United States, a platter of fruit is commonly accepted as a lunch dish, especially if served with cottage cheese.

Sometimes it comes in a pineapple shell which has been scooped and filled with fruit, and sometimes it is served in a large bowl or on a platter.

The fruit is usually mixed as for a fruit salad but an even better presentation can be made by preparing the fruits separately and arranging them in sections on a large platter. Not only is this more visually exciting but keeps the flavours separate.

As long as there are different colours and tastes any fruits in season can be used: berries, pineapple, nectarines, the various melons, pawpay (papaya), red or green grapes, apricots or mango. When fruit is becoming a little scarce, a selection of 3 or 4 can be used in larger quantities. But rely on fresh fruit, never use tinned.

The salad is served with a light orange sauce spooned over the top, and a little of this goes on the accompanying cottage cheese. Without the cheese the platter makes a marvellous dessert after a rich main course.

Quantities are a little difficult to specify, it depends not only on appetites but also on whether anything else is served. For lunch it should be ample for 6 to 8.

Serves 6–8	2 large yellow peaches
1 medium-sized mango	**3 medium-sized bananas**
1 medium-sized to small	**lemon juice**
melon or canteloupe	**500 g–750 g (1–1½ lb)**
4 oranges	**cottage cheese**
1 small pineapple	
2 Chinese gooseberries	Sauce:
(Kiwi fruit)	**rind of 2 oranges**
250 g (8 oz) seedless green	**1 cup (8 fl oz) orange juice**
grapes	**3 tablespoons sugar**
500 g (1 lb) strawberries	**1 tablespoon lemon juice**

Prepare all the fruit and chill it separately.

Skin the mango and cut into long thin slices, discarding the stone. Peel the melon or canteloupe and cut in half. Remove and discard the seeds. Cut into thin slices. Peel the orange, being careful to remove all white pith. Using a small sharp knife, take out the segments, leaving the membrane.

Cut away the skin from the pineapple. Cut in half and then into quarters. Remove the core and cut the flesh into thin slices. Do the same with the Chinese gooseberry, but don't leave this fruit for too long after it has been cut or it will become limp.

Remove all the grapes from the stalks. Wash the berries carefully or brush them with a pastry brush. You can hull them if you wish but they look nicer with their green tops.

Prepare the peach and banana as close to dinner time as you can. Peel and slice the peaches and add a little lemon juice. Stir gently to coat. Slice the banana, not too thinly, squeeze over a little lemon juice and toss.

Arrange all the fruit in sections on a large platter, overlapping the slices. Cover with plastic wrap and chill until serving time. The fruit can stand for an hour if refrigerated. You can add the sauce about 30 minutes before serving.

Place the cottage cheese in a mound, with some grape leaves around it or on pieces of lettuce, cover and chill. Sauce: Cut the orange peel into wafer thin slivers, using either a sharp knife or a zester. Put into a small saucepan. Cover generously with water and simmer until the peel is quite soft and tender. If the water boils down too much add more as it can take some time to cook to this stage. Drain.

Place into a pan with the orange juice and sugar and simmer again until the peel is translucent and the sauce reduced to about half. Remove from the heat and add the lemon juice. It should be slightly tart and fresh tasting. This sauce can be made several days in advance. About 1 tablespoon of the sauce is used to coat the cottage cheese—be sure to include some shreds of orange for colour. The rest of the sauce is spooned over the fruit.

Salad of Witlof, Radish and Apples

Serves 4	Dressing:
2 medium-sized heads of	**3 tablespoons vegetable oil**
witlof	**1 tablespoon lemon juice**
½ cup radish slices, cut	**1 tablespoon mayonnaise**
wafer-thin	**2 tablespoons thick cream**
2 medium-sized apples	
1 tablespoon lemon juice	
3 tablespoons roughly	
chopped walnuts	
8 slices ham	

Remove any yellow leafy parts from the witlof and cut the stalks into thick strips. Chill these in iced water.

Chill the radish.

Peel and core the apple and cut it into dice. Add lemon juice, turning so all the pieces are coated.

Place the witlof onto a platter or in a wide, shallow bowl. Scatter the drained radish on top. Spread the apple over this.

Mix all the dressing ingredients together, whisk well.

Cover the salad with the dressing and, with a fork, separate it slightly so that a little of the dressing seeps through to the base. Sprinkle with nuts.

Cut the ham slices in half and roll them up. Arrange these around, or on top of, the salad.

Gado Gado (page 60)

Curried Fruit in a Pineapple Shell with Chicken (page 61)

Fruit and Cottage Cheese Platter (page 62)

Lobster with Green dressing

The size of lobster you buy will depend on individual appetites and on what other courses are to be served.

If you can, buy small ones and put the flesh back in the shell. Alternatively, a very large lobster could be served on a platter, rather than in its shell, and covered with the green mayonnaise.

It is quite a rich dish, so if you wish to serve anything with it, keep it very simple.

Serves 4

Green mayonnaise:

$\frac{3}{4}$ **cup firmly packed, finely chopped fresh spinach**

$\frac{1}{2}$ **cup firmly packed watercress leaves**

2 tablespoons vegetable oil

$\frac{1}{3}$ **cup (2$\frac{1}{2}$ oz) mayonnaise**

2 tablespoons yogurt

1 medium-sized cucumber

salt and pepper

Lobster:

2 medium-sized lobsters

1 butter lettuce or 1 mignonette lettuce

4 medium-sized tomatoes, peeled

4 hard-boiled eggs

Place the spinach into a bowl and pour boiling water onto it. Let it stand for about 30 seconds; drain well. Refresh with some cold water.

Place the spinach and watercress leaves into either a blender or a food processor. (It may not be as successful in the processor as the quantity is small.)

Add the oil and blend until smooth. (If difficult to blend, mix in the mayonnaise, purée, then add the yogurt.) Mix with the mayonnaise and yogurt. Season with salt and pepper. Mix in the coral from the lobster.

Peel the cucumber, remove the seeds and grate enough to measure 1 cup: 1 oz. Salt lightly and let it stand for at least 30 minutes. Drain well, squeezing all the juice from the cucumber. Mix into the dressing.

Lobster: Cut each lobster in half, lengthwise. Remove the back intestinal vein, then slice the flesh into medium thick pieces. Reserve the coral or 'mustard' to use in the dressing.

Rinse the shell and dry it.

Place just a small spoonful of the dressing in the shell. Arrange the lobster pieces in the shell and spoon more dressing over the top.

Keep chilled if not serving immediately, but don't leave longer than 1 hour. It is better to keep the dressing separate, although the shellfish can be prepared well ahead.

Arrange the lobster shells on lettuce. Place to one side of each plate.

Cut the tomatoes and hard-boiled eggs into segments.

Arrange alternating segments of tomato and egg along the other side of the plate.

Mixed Shellfish salad

A salad made entirely of shellfish is an expensive but beautiful dish. My suggestions regarding the varieties and quantities should perhaps be regarded only as a guideline.

The scallops, prawns and mussels are in more or less equal proportions. These can be changed if you prefer more of one than the other, but try to use a selection of at least three varieties. Small rings of squid are also good as an addition, or pieces of lobster.

Most of the beauty of this salad lies in the absolute freshness of the taste, and in its presentation. All the ingredients can be chopped and left refrigerated, but mix them as close as possible to serving time. Even after 30 minutes of standing in the dressing everything becomes just slightly limp, and while the taste may be almost as good, it is disappointing if such a lovely salad isn't perfect to look at.

Serves 4

Shellfish Mixture:

250 g (8 oz) scallops

500 g (1 lb) prawns (jumbo shrimp)

24 fresh mussels

1 cup (8 fl oz) dry white wine

1 cup (8 fl oz) water

2 sprigs parsley

1 thin slice lemon

salt

few peppercorns

Salad:

1 medium-sized cucumber

salt

375 g (12 oz) ripe tomatoes, peeled

$\frac{1}{4}$ **cup finely chopped spring onions (scallions)**

1 cup finely chopped celery

1 medium-sized avocado

Dressing:

$\frac{1}{3}$ **cup (2$\frac{1}{2}$ fl oz) olive or vegetable oil**

1 tablespoon lemon juice

2 tablespoons finely chopped parsley

1 tablespoon finely chopped chives

2 tablespoons fresh basil

Clean the scallops. If the coral comes away, keep it as it adds colour to the dish.

Heat the wine and water with the parsley, lemon, salt and peppercorns. Simmer gently for about 3 minutes.

Add the scallops; don't let the water boil; simmer very gently for about 1 minute if small, 2 minutes if larger.

Remove with a slotted spoon and place on one plate, covering with another to keep them moist.

Wash the mussels and add to the liquid in which the scallops were cooked. Cover the pan and cook until the shells open. Remove immediately so they won't toughen. Remove the mussels from the shells.

Mix the scallops and mussels and add a few spoonfuls of liquid to moisten them. They can be stored in the refrigerator for several hours, but the longer they are kept the firmer they become.

Shell the prawns and cut in half, if you wish, or leave them whole. Cover and refrigerate.

Mix the shellfish with the dressing and salad only about 10 minutes before serving.

Salad: Peel the cucumber, cut in half lengthwise. Remove the seeds and dice the cucumber into chunky pieces. Cover with a little salt and let it stand for 30 minutes. Squeeze to remove all the moisture. If too salty, rinse, then drain and pat dry.

Cut the tomatoes into small pieces and discard the seeds and juice.

Mix the cucumber, tomatoes, spring onions and celery.

Peel the avocado and remove the stone. Either form small

balls with a melon baller, or cut into dice. Gently toss all the vegetables together in a large bowl.

Dressing: Mix the oil with the lemon juice, add the parsley and chives. Break the basil leaves into small pieces and add. Whisk with a fork or shake in a jar until thick.

Pour the dressing over the vegetables, folding all the shellfish in gently.

Serve on a large platter or in a shell-shaped dish or bowl.

Cucumber Prawn salad on a bed of Cabbage with Coconut

Chinese cabbage is the main ingredient in this salad. The raw shredded cabbage is mixed with a heated coconut sauce, which softens the strands slightly. You can either use tinned coconut milk, or make your own coconut milk from desiccated coconut (see page 60).

Chinese cabbage is used because it has a mild flavour, but if it is not easy to obtain, a very young, sweet plain cabbage could be used instead. Avoid strongly flavoured cabbage for this dish because it would overwhelm the subtle taste of the cucumber and prawns.

The cabbage can be prepared many hours beforehand, but assemble the salad only at the last moment.

As it is quite rich, it is adequate as a main dish. To serve as a first course, prepare only the cucumber and prawn salad.

Serves 4

Cabbage Salad:
2 cups finely shredded Chinese cabbage, firmly packed
$\frac{1}{2}$ cup (4 fl oz) coconut milk (see p. 60)
1 tablespoon sugar
2 tablespoons lemon juice
1 tablespoon Vietnamese fish sauce (see note)
black pepper

Note: Vietnamese fish sauce is made from anchovies and can be obtained in Oriental shops. If you like you can use 1 teaspoon of anchovy sauce instead.

Cucumber and Prawn:
2 medium-sized cucumbers, approximately 375 g (12 oz) each
salt
1 tablespoon sugar
750 g (1$\frac{1}{2}$ lb) cooked prawns, peeled
2 white onions
1 garlic clove
1 dried chilli
2 tablespoons vegetable oil
1 tablespoon lemon juice
1 teaspoon cumin
$\frac{1}{2}$ cup (4 oz) finely chopped peanuts

Place the cabbage into a bowl.

Heat the coconut milk, sugar, lemon juice and the Vietnamese fish sauce. Let it come to the boil and then pour it over the cabbage. Toss to coat the strands evenly. Add some pepper. The fish sauce is quite salty so you don't need to season with salt.

To make the cucumber and prawn salad, peel the cucumbers, score the sides and cut in half lengthwise.

Using a teaspoon, remove all the seeds. Cut the cucumber into wafer-thin slices. Place in a bowl with the salt and sugar and let it stand for at least 30 minutes.

Drain and squeeze the cucumber firmly, using your hands, to remove any excess moisture. Mix with the prawns.

Cut the onions in half and then into thin slices. Place into a frying pan, add the garlic, chilli and oil. Heat for a few minutes, stirring continuously, until the onion has softened slightly but don't allow them to brown.

Remove the garlic clove and chilli.

Add the lemon juice and cumin, and stir.

Fold the onion mixture into the prawns and cucumber, cover and keep chilled.

To assemble the salad, place the cabbage on a large platter. Spoon the cucumber and prawn mixture into the centre of the cabbage. Scatter the peanuts over the top.

Serve at once.

Cucumber Prawn salad on a bed of Cabbage with Coconut

Prawn salad in Tomato Shells

Tomato shells filled with a prawn salad, generously coated with mayonnaise, is not such an unusual dish; it is the presentation that lifts this one out of the ordinary.

The filled tomatoes are inverted onto the plate and wrapped with bands of green. It is easy to prepare and looks interesting.

I suggest using medium ripe tomatoes; one per person should be sufficient for a lunch, but a potato or rice dish could be added.

The best type of tomatoes to use for this dish are smooth ones; those that are convoluted or uneven would not be suitable because the 'bands of green' would not stick to the edges.

Serves 4

4 large firm, ripe tomatoes
salt and pepper
sugar
500 g (1 lb) cooked prawns
2 tablespoons finely
  chopped spring onions
  (scallions)
2 teaspoons finely chopped
  fresh dill
3 hard-boiled eggs, roughly
  chopped
alfalfa sprouts
$\frac{1}{2}$ bunch watercress

Garnish:

chives or spring onion tops
  and 8 sprigs parsley

Dressing:

$\frac{3}{4}$ cup (6 fl oz) mayonnaise
2 tablespoons lemon juice
1 tablespoon tomato sauce
  (ketchup)
salt and pepper
1 teaspoon Worcestershire
  sauce

The tomatoes need to be peeled carefully for this salad. Place them into a bowl and pour boiling water over them. Leave for about 10 seconds and then remove and place into cold water. Don't make the outside of the tomatoes soft or it will spoil their appearance.

Peel the skins away and cut the tomatoes in halves. Scoop out the seeds and most of the inside, leaving a shell. Season with salt, pepper and a pinch of sugar. Turn the tomatoes upside down to drain.

The tomatoes should be filled no more than an hour before serving but the prawn mixture can be made and stored, covered, in the refrigerator.

Mix together all the dressing ingredients.

Shell the prawns and chop into small pieces. Mix with the spring onions, dill, eggs and dressing. The mixture should be very moist.

Place the filling into the tomatoes, packing down gently so they are well filled. Turn the tomatoes upside down so the filled side is on the plate. Surround with some alfalfa sprouts.

Place the long chive pieces into a basin, or cut the ends of spring onions into long strips.

Pour boiling water over them to soften them slightly. Leave for a couple of minutes, then drain.

Arrange several of these long strands around each tomato half to form bands.

Place a sprig of parsley in the centre to cover the little root end of the tomato.

Break off the sprigs of watercress from their stems and arrange some on the sides of the alfalfa.

You could squeeze some lemon juice on the alfalfa if you like, but I find that once the tomatoes are cut, there is sufficient dressing to flavour the alfalfa.

Trout with Two sauces

Trout is a beautifully fine-textured fish, although perhaps a little light in flavour and bland at times, particularly when served cold.

It does present a lovely platter, however, and with this idea of two different coatings has plenty of flavour as a salad.

Probably the most important thing is not to overcook the fish; it should be very moist and sweet; trout which is left too long in the pan becomes very dry when cold.

This method of cooking the fish in a court bouillon and then wrapping it in foil to keep it moist is most successful.

Try to cook the fish in the afternoon if you are serving it for a dinner, or first thing in the morning for a lunch.

Have the trout boned if possible; most good fish shops will do this for you provided you order it ahead. If not, cook the fish with the bones in, but warn your guests beforehand.

A potato salad is good alongside the fish, or perhaps a light green salad as well.

Serves 4

4 rainbow trout, boned
1 cup (8 fl oz) white wine
1 cup (8 fl oz) water
several sprigs parsley,
  including the stems
1 teaspoon salt
4 black peppercorns

First Sauce:

$\frac{1}{2}$ cup (4 fl oz) oil
  mayonnaise
2 teaspoons Worcestershire
  sauce
2 teaspoons tomato paste
1 tablespoon finely
  chopped capers
lemon juice

Second Sauce:

$\frac{1}{4}$ cup watercress leaves,
  firmly packed
2 tablespoons finely
  chopped parsley
$\frac{1}{4}$ cup finely chopped sorrel
  leaves
2 tablespoons vegetable oil
1 teaspoon finely grated
  lemon rind
$\frac{1}{2}$ cup (4 fl oz) oil
  mayonnaise
1 teaspoon freshly grated
  horseradish or relish

Garnish:

Watercress sprigs
lemon slices

Season the trout lightly inside.

Place the wine, water, parsley, salt and peppercorns into a frying pan. Simmer gently for about 4 to 5 minutes, being careful not to let any liquid evaporate.

Add the trout; if the pan is not very large, it is best to cook only two at a time. Cook just a couple of minutes each side, turning them over once. Be very careful not to over-cook them.

Wrap gently in foil to keep moist until they are cool.

Remove the skin from the trout nearer to serving time, rather than too far ahead.

First Sauce: Mix the mayonnaise, Worcestershire sauce, tomato paste and capers. Add some lemon (it should be very fresh tasting and slightly tart). Chill until ready to use.

Second Sauce: Place the watercress and parsley into a bowl and pour boiling water over them. Drain and refresh under cold water.

Do the same with the sorrel.

Place into a food processor or a blender with the oil and mix until it forms a green purée. It doesn't matter if there are some specks in it; since it is not a large quantity it sometimes does not become very smooth.

Mix with the lemon rind, mayonnaise and horseradish. Taste for seasoning. Chill until ready to use.

Note: Both these sauces keep well for about 6 hours.

To assemble the salad, place the trout on a platter. Stir the First Sauce very well and spoon it down one side of the trout.

Stir the Second Sauce and use to cover the other side of the trout. This is easy to do because they are firm enough not to run together. If very thick, you can almost spread them on top.

Arrange some sprigs of watercress and a few slices of lemon around the fish. Serve within an hour.

Trout with Two sauces (above)

Honey-glazed Fish salad

A slightly sweet dish, its flavour is reminiscent of Chinese cooking.

Use a fine-textured fish, and one without bones, because it is difficult to see the bones when the fish is on a bed of lettuce.

I find flat fillets of whiting, John Dory, or flounder perfect for the recipe, but buy whatever is freshest on the day.

Taste the sauce when you make it and if you find it is too sweet, add a little extra lemon to freshen it.

The salad looks very attractive and served with an accompaniment of rice, is quite filling.

Serves 4
8 flat fillets of fish
plain flour
salt and pepper
30 g (1 oz) butter
1 tablespoon vegetable oil
Note: If the fillets of fish are large, you may need to make double the quantity of sauce.

Sauce:
2 tablespoons light brown
  sugar
2 tablespoons honey
$\frac{1}{3}$ cup ($2\frac{1}{2}$ fl oz) orange juice

1 tablespoon lemon juice
1 teaspoon grated fresh
  ginger
2 teaspoons arrowroot or
  cornflour (cornstarch)
8 lettuce leaves, finely
  shredded
2 tablespoons finely
  chopped spring onions
  (scallions)
2 oranges

Make sure there are no bones in the fish.

Mix the flour with salt and pepper and dust the fish lightly.

In a frying pan, heat the butter and oil and add the fish fillets. (If necessary, cook them in two batches so they can be handled without breaking.)

Cook the fish, turning once, until it is done. The fish will continue to cook slightly as it cools. Be careful not to over-cook it or it will become dry.

Drain on kitchen paper and then place on a platter, ready to coat with the sauce.

Once the fish is cooked, prepare the sauce immediately because it should be spooned onto the fish while the fish is still slightly warm.

In a small saucepan, heat the brown sugar and honey until it is melted and bubbling.

Add the orange juice, lemon juice and fresh ginger and simmer gently for a couple of minutes.

Mix the cornflour with a little water to form a paste and add to the hot sauce. Stir until it is slightly thick. It will become thicker as it cools.

Spoon or brush a layer of sauce over each fish fillet, continuing until all the sauce is finished. Spoon over any sauce that flows onto the plate while the fish is cooling.

You can cover and refrigerate the fish if necessary, but serve it at room temperature.

Arrange fish fillets on top of lettuce, placing finely chopped spring onion alongside.

Remove the skin and outside white pith from the oranges and cut out segments, leaving all the membrane behind. Arrange three segments on top of each fish fillet.

Prawn salad in Tomato Shells (page 68)

Smoked Mackerel and Egg salad (page 73)

Fish Fillets with Spiced Tomato dressing (page 72)

Whole Baked Fish with mayonnaise

Among the presentation of cold fish dishes, probably the most impressive of all is to have a whole fish assembled and garnished on a platter and then served at the table.

I hesitate to name a fish because of the huge variations which exist, not only in different countries, but also in different states.

The best guarantee of quality and freshness will be the recommendations of your local fish supplier. But it must be whole, not a section of fish. Neither must it be frozen.

Regardless of the types I have used, this method of cooking the fish, then wrapping it tightly in a piece of foil, ensures beautiful, moist flesh every time.

Serves 4

$\frac{1}{2}$ cup (4 fl oz) dry white wine
4 cups (1 litre) water
1 bay leaf
1 small onion, cut into thick slices
few leaves from the top of celery
sprig of thyme
1 clove garlic, left whole
1 teaspoon salt
1 fish weighing approximately 750 g ($1\frac{1}{2}$ lb)

Jellied Mayonnaise:

1 cup (8 fl oz) oil mayonnaise
2 tablespoons tomato sauce (ketchup)
1 tablespoon lemon juice
2 teaspoons horseradish relish
2 teaspoons gelatine
2 tablespoons water

Salad:

1 lettuce, either mignonette or butter
1 very small cucumber
8 slices lemon, cut wafer-thin
some watercress sprigs

Place the wine, water, bay leaf, onion, celery, thyme, garlic and salt into a saucepan and simmer gently for about 10 minutes. Don't let the liquid evaporate. You can prepare this at any stage, even the day before but cook the fish on the day it is to be eaten so it will be as moist as possible.

Place the liquid into a baking tin large enough to accommodate the fish easily. Bring the liquid to the boil and place the fish into it. Cover with a piece of foil, thickly buttered. Cook in a very slow oven; the liquid should be barely trembling.

Cooking time will depend on the thickness of the fish rather than its weight, but between 10 to 15 minutes should be sufficient. It will continue to cook after it is removed from the oven so don't overcook in the beginning.

Remove from the liquid, wrap tightly in foil while hot and leave to become cold.

Unwrap the fish carefully. Remove all the skin. Place the fish onto a platter or a piece of foil from which it can be easily transferred.

Spoon the mayonnaise (see below) over the fish (you will probably need to do this in several layers); the first layer may not coat it evenly. Place in the refrigerator until just set, then coat again.

Leave the fish refrigerated, but not for too long as the flesh becomes firmer the colder it becomes.

Jellied Mayonnaise: Mix the mayonnaise with the tomato sauce, lemon and horseradish.

Mix the gelatine with the water and stir to incorporate any dry bits.

Place into a cup and stand it in a saucepan of water over a moderate heat until the gelatine is clear.

Remove and add a few spoonfuls of the mayonnaise to the gelatine.

Return the mixture to the bowl and leave to stand until it is just cool. It can set very quickly, depending on whether or not the mayonnaise has been refrigerated, so have the fish ready to coat.

Salad: Chill the lettuce. Peel the cucumber in strips, leaving some of the skin on. Cut it in half lengthwise, then into thin slices.

Cut the lemon slices in half.

Place the watercress sprigs in the refrigerator to crisp.

Arrange butter lettuce on a platter and place the fish in the centre.

Place overlapping slices of cucumber all around. You can season them with a little oil and vinegar, if you wish, or leave them plain.

Decorate with the lemon slices and watercress sprigs.

Fish Fillets with Spiced Tomato dressing

Any very fine-textured white fish can be used for this dish. Use flat fillets rather than thick, chunky pieces. Whiting, for example, is ideal, or baby John Dory, but buy whatever is freshest in this type of fish.

All the bones must be removed because they are difficult to find in a salad where the fish is covered in sauce.

The dish can be quickly made and the sauce is slightly spiced but the flavour is not so strong that it overwhelms the fish.

You need to have ripe tomatoes; floury ones will not give a successful result.

All that is needed to accompany the fish is a bowl of small potatoes, and perhaps a plain green salad.

Serves 4

8 fish fillets, each weighing approximately 75 g ($3\frac{1}{2}$ oz)
$\frac{1}{2}$ cup (4 fl oz) dry white wine
$\frac{1}{2}$ cup (4 fl oz) water
salt
8 lettuce leaves
$\frac{1}{2}$ bunch watercress

Dressing:

250 g (8 oz) ripe tomatoes, peeled
$\frac{1}{2}$ white onion, finely diced
1 teaspoon sugar
$\frac{1}{3}$ cup ($2\frac{1}{2}$ fl oz) vegetable oil
2 teaspoons Worcestershire sauce
2 tablespoons lemon juice
salt and pepper

In a frying pan, heat the wine, water and salt. When it comes to the boil, add the fish fillets. Cook only a few at a time so as not to crowd the pan.

Turn the fillets over once and poach over low heat until just cooked. Be sure not to overcook them or they will become dry.

Remove the fillets as soon as they are cooked and carefully scrape off any dark skin that remains. Place into a shallow dish.

To make the dressing, cut the tomatoes into very tiny pieces, crushing them slightly with the back of a knife and discarding some of the juice and seeds. It should be a thickish pulp, not watery. Place the pulp in a bowl, add the onion, sugar, oil, Worcestershire sauce and lemon juice and season well with salt and pepper.

Pour the dressing over the fish and leave for at least 1 hour; but it can be left to marinate for 5 to 6 hours. If the weather is warm, place the dish in the refrigerator but do not allow the fish to become too cold or the flesh will become firm and some flavour will be lost.

To assemble the salad, place several lettuce leaves on individual plates, arrange the drained fish on the lettuce and spoon some of the dressing on top. Place some sprigs of watercress on the side of the fish.

Fillets of Fish Escabeche

This salad of pickled fish comes from Spain.

It is quite highly flavoured, as is much Spanish food, with a marinade that soaks into the cooked fish while it is cooling. During this time, the flavour will become more subtle, and the vinegar and wine, which will have a strong smell while the mixture is cooking, will mellow.

Most of the recipes recommend that the dish be prepared 24 hours before it is to be eaten but I find it becomes rather firm and dry and much prefer to eat it on the day it is made.

Almost any type of fish can be used, provided it is properly filleted, but be sure not to overcook the fish when frying it.

Serves 4

3 tablespoons olive oil
2 medium-sized white onions, cut into thin slices
1 cup grated carrot
1 small green pepper (capsicum), seeds removed and cut into thin strips
$\frac{1}{2}$ cup (4 fl oz) water
$\frac{1}{2}$ cup (4 fl oz) dry white wine
1 bay leaf
1 clove garlic, finely chopped or crushed
1 teaspoon finely chopped fresh chilli
$\frac{1}{2}$ teaspoon salt
pepper
$\frac{1}{4}$ cup (2 fl oz) white wine vinegar
500 g (1 lb) fillets of fish
plain flour
additional oil to cook the fish

Heat the oil in a saucepan. Add the onion, grated carrot and pepper and fry over medium heat, stirring occasionally, for about 5 minutes or until the vegetables have softened slightly.

Add the water, wine, bay leaf, garlic, chilli, salt, pepper and vinegar and simmer gently for another 5 minutes. Don't allow it to boil or you will lose too much liquid.

Dust the fish lightly with flour.

Heat sufficient oil to barely cover the base of a frying pan and cook the fish, turning it once. Don't overcook it or it will become too firm when cold.

If the marinade has become cold, warm it again quickly because it should be used while it is hot.

Place half the marinade in the base of a glass or china dish large enough to take the fish in one layer.

Arrange the fillets of fish in the marinade and then pour the rest of the marinade over the fish. Spread the vegetables so they cover the fish evenly.

Allow it to cool, cover tightly, and leave to stand for at least 6 hours before eating.

Smoked Mackerel and Egg salad

Displayed in the shops, the dark, hard skin of a smoked mackerel gives little indication of the lovely, moist flesh underneath. It has a satisfying but very rich flavour and is good served in chunky pieces on a portion of buttered bread or toast. It is also ideal for salads.

I find that mackerel is most suitable for this dish but if you prefer you could use any smoked fish, provided it is moist. Occasionally some smoked fish are dry, especially trout, so be a little cautious when choosing the fish.

The fish can be mixed with the dressing hours beforehand, but assemble the salad at the last moment or the lettuce will become limp.

Serves 4
Note: The portions may seem small, but the fish is very rich so a little is sufficient.
500 g (1 lb) smoked mackerel or trout
6 hard-boiled eggs
lettuce leaves
watercress or small sprigs of chicory (endive)
2 tablespoons spring onions (scallions), roughly chopped
4 nasturtium flowers

Dressing:
6 tablespoons vegetable oil
2 tablespoons white wine vinegar
1 teaspoon grated horseradish
1 tablespoon sour cream

Discard the firm outside skin of the fish and then lift off the flesh in small pieces, being careful to remove any bones.

Cut the hard-boiled eggs in half lengthwise and then into quarters.

Place sufficient lettuce leaves to lightly cover the base of a large platter. Sprinkle spring onions over the top of the lettuce.

Whisk all the ingredients for the dressing together, except the sour cream. Spoon about half the sour cream over the bed of lettuce and mix the remainder into the dressing.

Pour the dressing over the fish and toss gently, adding a little salt or pepper as needed.

Heap the fish in the centre of the platter and surround with the egg sections. Decorate with watercress or sprigs of pale green pieces of chicory.

Remove the petals from the flowers and place a petal on top of each egg section.

Lobster with Green dressing (page 66)

Mixed Shellfish salad (page 66)

Honey-glazed Fish salad (page 69)

Smoked Fish salad

I once heard somebody describe smoked fish as being at the lower end of the social scale of the fish industry.

It seems a strange statement because smoked fish is not necessarily cheaper, but perhaps the inferior quality smoked fish, where the flavour is destroyed by saltiness or dryness, has given it a poor name. Good quality smoked fish is excellent.

Used in salad it is unusual, with a distinctive smoky flavour, and an added freshness is given with the inclusion of celery and cucumber.

Be sure to buy a plump, top quality product and don't overcook the fish because as it cools it continues to cook and will become dry.

This is quite a simple salad but you could put some slices or wedges of hard-boiled egg on top for added interest.

The smoky flavour is perfect served with a bowl of potatoes as a side dish.

Serves 4

$\frac{1}{2}$ cup (4 fl oz) milk	Dressing:
$\frac{3}{4}$ cup (6 fl oz) water	$\frac{1}{2}$ cup (4 fl oz) vegetable oil
500 g (1 lb) smoked fish	2 tablespoons lemon juice
1 cup finely sliced celery	1 tablespoon finely
1 cucumber, 375 g (12 oz)	chopped capers
salt	1 tablespoon finely
1 white onion, finely diced	chopped parsley
1 mignonette or butter	1 tablespoon finely
lettuce	chopped fresh dill
few sprigs of dill, to	
garnish	

Heat the milk and water in a frying pan. Add the fish, cover the pan and simmer gently, turning the fish once, until it is just tender and flakes when touched.

Remove, and cover with a plate to keep it moist.

Place the celery into iced water until it is crisp.

Peel the cucumber and cut it lengthwise. Using a teaspoon, remove the seeds. Cut the cucumber into dice and sprinkle it with salt. Let it stand for at least 30 minutes, then drain away the liquid. Rinse the cucumber and drain again thoroughly.

Mix the drained celery with the cucumber and onion.

Flake the fish, being very careful to remove any remaining bones.

To make the dressing, mix the oil, lemon juice, capers, parsley and dill. Whisk, or shake in a jar, until thickened. Check the seasoning before adding salt because the smoked fish will be slightly salty. Add pepper if you wish.

Add the fish to the celery and cucumber and stir in the dressing. Allow to stand for 1 hour to marinate.

Arrange the lettuce around the edge of a platter and heap the salad in the centre. Decorate with sprigs of fresh dill.

Warm Seafood salad

One of the first 'warm salads' I ever tasted was in France at the Chateau St Martin, a luxurious hotel in Provence.

Perched like an eagle on the side of the mountain, the chateau overlooks the lavender- and thyme-carpeted valleys beneath.

It is run by a young Frenchwoman, Andre Brunet, and the menu she chose for my lunch included this dish as the first course.

Local fish from the Mediterranean were used in the salad and after placing the pieces of fish on a base of different kinds of lettuce, a squeeze of lemon was added. It was a beautiful dish, fresh and moist, and I was completely captivated by the entire concept.

This recipe is not from the chateau, for I was not given one, but the directions for preparing this style of salad were explained.

I have altered the original idea slightly and instead of the lemon, a light dressing is used. However, this is optional.

Serves 4

250 g (8 oz) scallops	Dressing:
250 g (8 oz) fillets of fish	3 tablespoons vegetable oil
250 g (8 oz) shelled green	2 tablespoons lemon juice
prawns	1 teaspoon pink
flour	peppercorns
salt and pepper	salt and pepper
mignonette or butter	
lettuce	
watercress	
some oil to cook the fish	
a few long strips of chives,	
to garnish	

Clean the scallops, removing the dark section on the side. Separate the coral if you wish but keep this to use in the dish.

Cut the fish into thin strips, making sure there are no bones remaining.

Remove the dark vein from the prawns.

Select about 16 lettuce leaves for the salad and break off the watercress sprigs from the heavy stalks. You will need about 16 to 24 sprigs of watercress. Chill both the lettuce and the cress.

Just before cooking the fish, arrange the lettuce and cress on individual plates, placing the stalk end of the lettuce towards the centre and the watercress around the edge of the plates.

Heat sufficient oil in two pans to coat the base with a thin layer. Dust the fish lightly with some flour which has been seasoned with salt and pepper. Shake off any excess flour.

Place the fish in one pan, the prawns in the other, and cook for a couple of minutes, turning them over so that they cook evenly.

Push the fish to one side and add the scallops to the same pan, turning them over as you cook them.

Cook only for a minute for tiny scallops, several minutes if larger. Place all the seafood on kitchen paper to drain.

To make the dressing, place the oil and lemon either into a jar or whisk in a bowl until thick. Wash the peppercorns to make the taste milder, drain well, and add with some salt and pepper.

Arrange the seafood on the lettuce, giving each person a selection, and then spoon a little of the dressing on top, dividing the peppercorns evenly. Scatter a few long strips of chives over the top, and serve immediately.

Warm Seafood salad

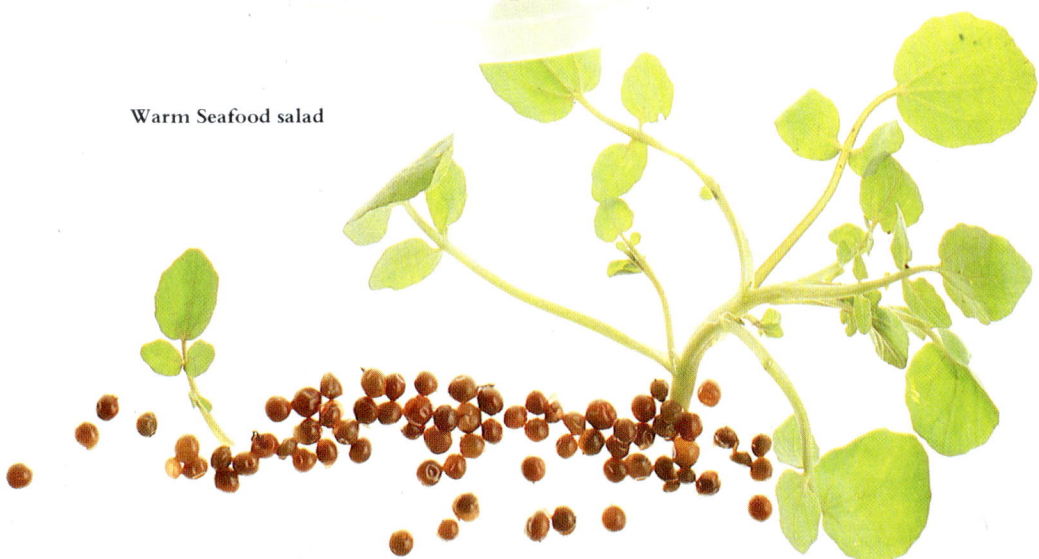

Simple Beef salad

The best meat for this, although the most expensive, is fillet of beef. But whatever beef you use, it must be very rare because even though it will change colour in the marinade, well-cooked meat will be firm and hard, underdone meat will become meltingly tender.

Because it is very well-flavoured, it can be made beforehand and refrigerated and still taste excellent. Remove from the refrigerator shortly before serving so it is not too cold.

This is a substantial salad but you would probably need to serve a side dish to accompany it—potatoes or pasta salad are both good.

Serves 4

750 g (1½ lb) rare roast beef	Dressing:
1 medium-sized white	½ cup (4 fl oz) olive oil
onion	2 teaspoons sugar
1 butter lettuce, radicchio	2 tablespoons white
lettuce or mignonette	vinegar
lettuce	2 teaspoons dry, hot
500 g (1 lb) ripe tomatoes	English-style mustard
several sweet-sour	2 teaspoons horseradish
cucumbers, to garnish	relish
	2 tablespoons finely
	chopped pickled
	cucumber

Remove any fat from the beef. Cut it into thin slices and then into pieces about 4 cm × 1 cm (1½ inches × ½ inch).

Cut the onion in half, then into very thin slices and separate the pieces. Mix with the beef.

To make the dressing, mix the oil, sugar and vinegar with the mustard, horseradish relish and cucumber. Whisk or stir well or shake in a jar until thick. (If you make it beforehand, stir again before adding to the beef.)

Add the dressing, stirring it well to coat the beef. Leave to stand for at least 1 hour. If you need to store it for some time, cover and refrigerate.

Arrange the lettuce around the edge of a shallow bowl.

Cut the tomatoes into thin slices and arrange around the lettuce, overlapping the slices.

Heap the beef salad in the centre of the tomato.

Slice the sweet-sour cucumbers thinly and arrange them in a fan shape over the top.

Beef salad Parisienne

This is one of the great traditional French dishes. It is so good that although it may originally have been created to make use of leftover beef, it warrants cooking some especially for the salad.

It is important to use rare beef, whether roasted or boiled; just make sure it is pink and juicy and it will retain these qualities in the finished dish. Meat that is well done makes a very dry salad.

It keeps well for a short time, chilled, so if you prepare it ahead of time, cover well before refrigerating. Be sure to remove it from the refrigerator a little while before serving because the flavour diminishes if it is too cold.

You can serve it with some crusty bread or add another small salad, such as cucumber, if you feel it needs an accompaniment.

The garnish on the beef can be as simple or as elaborate as you wish; some hard-boiled egg quarters, sprigs of herbs, a sprinkling of parsley or chives, or strips of sweet-sour cucumber.

Serves 4–6

500 g (1 lb) small potatoes	Dressing:
750 g (1½ lb) rare roast beef	¾ cup (6 fl oz) oil
1 large white or	¼ cup (2 fl oz) white wine
Spanish-style onion	vinegar
4 hard-boiled eggs	salt and pepper
1 butter or mignonette	1 tablespoon French
lettuce	mustard
2 tomatoes, cut into wedges	¼ cup finely chopped
	parsley
	1 tablespoon finely
	chopped chives
	2 tablespoons finely
	chopped sweet-sour
	cucumber
	¼ cup (2 fl oz) mayonnaise

Cook the potatoes, in their skins, in salted water until tender. Drain and when cool enough to handle remove the skins. Dice neatly.

Remove any fat from the beef and cut it into thin slices and then into strips.

Cut the onion in half and then into wafer-thin slices.

Cut the eggs into small pieces.

Make the dressing by mixing the oil and vinegar with the remaining dressing ingredients. Shake in a jar until thick.

Mix the potatoes, beef, onion and egg with the dressing. Toss until all the ingredients are well coated.

If you need to refrigerate the mixture, cover well and remove about 1 hour beforehand so it returns to room temperature.

To serve, arrange the lettuce around the edge of a platter. Mound the beef in the centre and arrange the tomato wedges on the edge of the beef.

Garnish with some parsley, or, if you like, add some quarters of hard-boiled eggs.

Spicy Oriental Beef salad

This Oriental-style salad has the addition of the slightly salty Vietnamese sauce and Vietnamese mint leaves, which taste a little like fresh coriander, sometimes known as Chinese parsley.

The salad has a little chilli but it is not particularly hot, although this could be adjusted if you wish.

The dish has a lovely fresh taste and needs perhaps only some rice on the side if you wish to serve an accompaniment.

Serves 4

500 g (1 lb) fillet, or top	¼ teaspoon Tabasco
quality grilling steak	4 Vietnamese mint leaves,
2 tablespoons vegetable oil	finely chopped
½ cup finely chopped	125 g (4 oz) bean shoots
spring onions (scallions)	1 small cucumber
2 tablespoons lemon juice	1 medium-sized red or
2 cloves garlic, crushed	green pepper (capsicum)
1 tablespoon sugar	8 lettuce leaves
1 tablespoon Vietnamese	few fresh sprigs Vietnamese
fish sauce	mint
1 teaspoon finely chopped	
fresh chilli or	

Cut the meat into long, wafer-thin slices, then each one into pieces about 4 cm (1½ inches) long.

Heat the oil and brown the meat over high heat, stirring constantly, until it has just changed colour on the outside. It should take only a couple of minutes; take care not to overcook it. It is sometimes better to cook the meat in two batches so that it can be turned more easily.

Place the meat into a basin and add the spring onions, lemon juice, garlic, sugar, fish sauce, chilli and chopped mint. Leave to marinate for about 1 hour. If leaving for longer, cover, and refrigerate but remove from the refrigerator at least an hour before serving.

Pinch the ends from the bean shoots and pour boiling water over them. Let them stand 30 seconds. Drain and chill.

Peel the cucumber. Cut it in half lengthwise, then into thin slices. Chill them.

Cut the pepper in half, remove the seeds and cut it into fine, long strips.

Wash the lettuce and put it in the refrigerator to crisp.

To serve, arrange the meat on one side of a platter, place the lettuce on the other side and make separate mounds of bean shoots and cucumber. Decorate with little piles of pepper and a few mint sprigs.

Cabbage and Corned Beef salad

Cabbage and corned beef is a famous, old-fashioned combination, served steaming hot with some mustard on chilly evenings.

This salad version bears no resemblance at all in flavour; it is a much lighter dish with the raw, shredded cabbage and potatoes surrounding the corned beef.

You could serve it with some mustard and crusty bread, if you wish, although it has sufficient flavour of its own.

You can buy the corned beef ready cooked, but be sure it is very moist and fresh and that it has not been sliced early in the day and allowed to dry out.

Serves 4

2 cups cabbage, very finely shredded
500 g (1 lb) small new potatoes
1 tablespoon white onion, finely chopped
⅓ cup grated carrot
18 thin slices corned beef
2 hard-boiled eggs, finely chopped
2 tablespoons sweet pickled cucumber, finely chopped

Dressing:

1 cup (8 fl oz) vegetable or olive oil
3 tablespoons white vinegar
1 tablespoon, dry, hot English-style mustard
pepper
2 tablespoons mayonnaise

Cook the potatoes, in their jackets, in salted water. Remove and when cool enough to handle, peel and cut them in quarters, or eighths, according to their size. Place in a bowl.

To make the dressing, place the oil and vinegar in a bowl or a jar and whisk or shake to mix. Add a little to the dry mustard and mix to a paste. Mix with the rest of the oil and vinegar and add some pepper. Don't add salt because the corned beef is usually slightly salty.

Set aside ⅓ cup (2½ fl oz) of the dressing to spoon over the corned beef. Add the mayonnaise to the remainder, mixing thoroughly before using.

Mix the cabbage with the potatoes and add the onion, carrot and the portion of dressing that has the mayonnaise. Allow to stand for at least 1 hour so the cabbage will soften slightly; you can leave it longer if you wish. Taste, and add salt if necessary.

To assemble, arrange the vegetables around the edge of a large platter. Place the corned beef slices, overlapping, down the centre. Spoon the remaining dressing over the corned beef. Scatter the chopped eggs over the top and then, finally, the pickled cucumber.

The salad can be covered and left for a short time before serving.

Spicy Oriental Beef salad (above)

Beef Rolls with Vegetable Batons (page 82)

Simple Beef salad (page 78)

Pork salad with Water Chestnuts (page 87)

Hot Steak salad

It is perhaps a little unusual to make a salad with fillet steak, but although it is cooked at the last moment, by the time it is served it will not be piping hot, just warm, and will have a fresh, moist flavour.

Be sure to use very good quality steak. The sauce could be made during the day and the meat cut, so the entire procedure need only take a few minutes before dinner.

Serve crusty bread on the side and you have a complete meal.

Serves 4

**500 g (1 lb) trimmed fillet
  steak**
black pepper
8 lettuce leaves
small handful of endive
2 ripe avocados
a little lemon juice
2 tablespoons vegetable oil

Sauce:
**⅓ cup cooked spinach, well
  drained**
**2 teaspoons grated white
  onion**

**1 teaspoon hot, dry
  English-style mustard**
1 teaspoon sugar
**1 teaspoon finely chopped
  capers**
**1 teaspoon grated
  horseradish**
3 tablespoons vegetable oil
**1 tablespoon white wine
  vinegar**
⅓ cup (2½ fl oz) mayonnaise

Trim every bit of fat and any sinew from the steak. Cut the meat into bite-sized pieces. Scatter them with some black pepper. Toss to coat and leave aside.

Break the lettuce leaves into a few pieces and place around the edge of dinner plates.

Cut the avocados in half, twisting each half to remove it from the stone. Peel and cut into thin slices.

Arrange the slices over the lettuce and squeeze a little lemon juice on top to prevent discolouration. It is best to do this just before cooking the steak.

Heat the oil in a frying pan. When very hot, add the cubes of steak and toss them so they cook evenly on the outside. Keep the steak pink inside for the best flavour.

Remove the meat and place on kitchen paper to drain, then place in the centre of the lettuce and avocado.

To make the sauce, chop the spinach very small. If you use frozen spinach, this will already be in either a purée or small pieces, but be sure it is well drained.

Add the onion, mustard, sugar, capers, horseradish, oil and vinegar and, lastly, mix in the mayonnaise.

Cover and chill if you make this beforehand but remove from the refrigerator about 30 minutes before using so it will come to room temperature.

Coat the meat with sauce, and serve.

Beef Rolls with Vegetable Batons

The 'batons' referred to in this recipe are little pieces of vegetable, cut slightly thicker than julienne strips.

It is a colourful and attractive dish which can be prepared and left to stand for about 6 hours.

Don't serve it too cold, and add the chive dressing only about 30 minutes before serving the dish.

Serves 4
Beef Rolls:
**500 g (1 lb) after trimming,
  fillet of beef**
black pepper
**2 teaspoons horseradish
  relish**
2 tablespoons mayonnaise
1 teaspoon mango chutney
**strips of sweet-sour pickled
  cucumber**

Vegetable Salad:
**1 large or 2 small beetroots
  (beets)**
2 medium-sized carrots
2 medium-sized zucchini
1 red pepper
1 medium-sized cucumber

Dressing:
**1 tablespoon French or
  Dijon mustard**
½ cup (4 fl oz) vegetable oil
2 tablespoon lemon juice
1 teaspoon sugar
**2 tablespoons finely
  chopped chives**

Beef Rolls: Place the trimmed fillet into a fairly hot oven, 220°C (400°F/Gas 6) and bake for about 20 minutes depending on the thickness of the meat.

Remove and wrap in foil until cool. It will continue cooking during this time so be very careful not to overcook it. The meat should be quite pink inside.

When cooled, slice as thinly as possible. Place on a board and, using either a large vegetable or chopping knife, or the palm of your hand, press down to flatten out the slices a little so the meat is quite fine and thin. Season with pepper.

Mix the horseradish, mayonnaise and chutney and spread a thin layer on the slices of meat. Place a strip of the pickled cucumber on top and roll over to enclose. The beef rolls can be prepared well ahead, covered tightly, and refrigerated.

Vegetable Salad: Cook the beetroot in a saucepan of lightly salted water until tender. Remove, cool and rub away the outside skin under cold, running water.

Cut into batons, or thick julienne strips.

Peel the carrot and cut into strips the same size. Cook until just tender.

Cut the zucchini in the same way and cook about 2 minutes. Drain, refresh with cold water.

Cut the pepper into fine strips, discarding the seeds. Place into cold water, bring to the boil and then drain.

Peel the cucumber, cut in half lengthwise, remove the seeds and cut the cucumber into strips.

Keep all the vegetables in small, separate bowls, tightly covered, until close to serving time.

Arrange the beef rolls on a platter, placing them on a bed of lettuce or, if you wish, serve a lettuce salad separately.

Arrange the different ingredients in little bundles around the beef, spoon the dressing over the top of the vegetables only, leaving the beef plain.

To make the dressing, mix the mustard with the oil, add the lemon juice and sugar and either shake in a jar or whisk until thick. Add the chives just before using. Leave aside if not using immediately.

Serve within 30 minutes, once the dressing has been added.

Chopped Beef salad

The Dutch have a national dish called 'Hussar Salad' which was a favourite of the Hussars when they invaded the Netherlands.

All the ingredients are chopped into small pieces, mixed well and then left for the flavours to mature. This salad is slightly different but is based on a similar theme and despite the chopping and mixing, the various ingredients still retain their identity.

Be sure to use rare beef. Although its appearance won't be noticed in the salad, its taste will be. The rare beef makes a moist salad; well-done meat becomes dry.

I like to use a fillet steak or similar quality meat, but whatever you use, trim it well of any fat or sinew.

Although this is a complete meal, you can accompany it with a green salad if you wish.

I like to use fresh beetroot but if you use tinned beetroot, drain it thoroughly or there will be too much vinegar in the finished dish.

Serves 4
- 250 g (8 oz) small potatoes
- 185 g (6 oz) small button mushrooms
- 1 tablespoon peanut oil
- salt and pepper
- 1 large white onion, cut into thin half-rings
- 500 g (1 lb) rare beef
- $\frac{1}{2}$ cup finely sliced celery
- 250 g (8 oz) beetroot (beets)
- 2 tablespoons chopped sweet-sour pickles
- 2 hard-boiled eggs, roughly chopped
- lettuce

Dressing:
- $\frac{3}{4}$ cup (6 fl oz) vegetable or olive oil
- 2 tablespoons red wine vinegar
- 2 tablespoons finely chopped parsley
- 2 teaspoons Worcestershire sauce
- 1 tablespoon finely chopped chives
- 1 teaspoon finely chopped fresh thyme
- salt and pepper

Garnish:
- $\frac{1}{2}$ cup (4 fl oz) cream
- 1 tablespoon horseradish relish
- 1 hard-boiled egg, very finely chopped

Cook the potatoes in their skins, cool and peel, then cut into medium-sized dice.

Cut the mushrooms in half, if they are not small ones, removing stalks if they are woody or fibrous.

Heat the oil in a frying pan, add the mushrooms, season and sauté about 1 minute over high heat until just barely softened.

Add the onion and cook another minute. It won't become soft but some of the strong flavour will be removed.

Trim the beef of any fat and cut it into thin slices, then each slice into long strips.

Mix the potatoes, mushrooms, onion and beef with the celery, pickles and eggs and fold through the dressing.

To make the dressing, mix the oil with all the remaining ingredients and either whisk or shake in a jar until thick.

The mixture can be left for about 6 hours but the beetroot is best added shortly before serving. Drain the beetroot thoroughly, cut it into small pieces or dice and mix it through carefully. (The mixture will become quite red.)

Chopped Beef salad (opposite)

To assemble, arrange the lettuce leaves on a round platter, to form a cupped circle.

Spoon the beef salad onto this, mounding it slightly to form an inverted basin shape.

Whip the cream lightly until it holds very soft peaks. Don't whip it too much or it will become too stiff. Add the horseradish.

Spread the horseradish cream over the top part of the salad. Press the finely chopped egg around the edge of the cream.

Once the cream is on the salad serve within 1 hour or it will become pink.

Salad of Two Meats

Beef and ham together may not sound compatible, but the smoky flavour of leg ham combined with the vegetables and slices of beef is very tasty.

This is a good way to use up the leftover ham from Christmas when you need to relieve the monotony of ham salads.

Small pieces of ham could be used, even the pieces that inevitably are left when large sections of ham are sliced. Remove some of the fat if the ham has a thick layer.

Be sure the beef is underdone for this salad; well-done beef becomes dry if allowed to stand. If you prefer, you could make this salad with either beef or ham alone.

Serves 4

500 g (1 lb) small new
  potatoes
3 medium-sized green or
  red peppers (capsicums)
1 large white or Spanish
  onion, cut in thin
  half-circles
250 g (8 oz) ham
250 g (8 oz) rare roast beef
butter or mignonette
  lettuce
watercress

Dressing:

375 g (12 oz) ripe tomatoes,
  peeled
1 teaspoon sugar
$\frac{1}{2}$ cup (4 fl oz) olive oil
2 tablespoons red wine
  vinegar
2 tablespoons finely
  chopped parsley
1 tablespoon finely
  chopped chives
2 tablespoons mayonnaise

Place the potatoes, unpeeled, into salted water and cook until tender. Drain. Leave to cool slightly so they can be easily handled. Peel the potatoes and cut into slices.

While the potatoes are cooking, prepare the peppers. Cut them in half, remove the seeds and place under the griller (broiler) until they are brown and the skin has blistered. Remove and cool slightly then peel away as much of the skin as you can. (It will be as thin as cellophane paper.)

Cut the peppers into small pieces.

Mix the potatoes and peppers together.

While the potatoes are warm, stir in the dressing. There will be an excess of dressing, although much soaks into the potatoes.

To make the dressing, cut the tomatoes into small pieces. Place them in a saucepan with the sugar and cook over medium heat for a few minutes or until the mixture is slightly thick. If a lot of liquid forms, and this depends on the amount of juice in the tomatoes, boil it away.

Remove and place into a bowl. Leave to cool a little. Add the oil, vinegar, parsley and chives and whisk until thick.

Add the mayonnaise and taste for seasoning. (The dressing can be made some time beforehand, but stir again before using.)

You can add the onions and meat now or later—it doesn't matter, as long as the potatoes are allowed to marinate for at least an hour before serving.

Mix in the onions, and stir.

Cut the ham into long strips.

Cut the beef into thin slices and then cut each slice in half.

Mix everything together, cover and leave to stand, stirring again before using.

You can chill the salad if keeping for more than a couple of hours, but remove from the refrigerator at least 1 hour before serving or it will not be as tasty. It must be eaten on the day it is made.

To serve, arrange a layer of lettuce around the outside of an oval platter. Heap the salad in the centre.

Remove the sprigs from the watercress and arrange these in a band around the edge of the salad.

Salad of Two Meats (above)

Lamb and Rice salad

Any leftover lamb can be used in this salad; a piece of meat such as leg of lamb, for example, is perfect, provided it is still pink and moist. If you wish to roast a piece of meat especially, you can buy a small half leg of lamb. There is too much wastage on other portions, such as a loin, because of the trimming required.

Take care to remove all the fat; it is unpleasant if left in the salad.

For this dish, the meat is marinated and develops a slightly sweet, minted flavour.

Serves 4

500 g (1 lb) rare cooked
  lamb
2 tablespoons redcurrant
  jelly
2 tablespoons finely
  chopped mint
2 tablespoons lemon juice
$\frac{1}{2}$ cup (4 fl oz) orange juice
2 tablespoons vegetable oil

1 finely chopped white
  onion
1 cup (8 oz) long-grain rice
2 cups (16 fl oz) chicken
  stock
1 sprig mint
1 cinnamon stick
125 g (4 oz) peas, shelled
$\frac{1}{2}$ cup sliced carrot
fresh mint sprigs, to garnish

Remove all the fat from the lamb and cut into thin slices.

Heat the jelly, mint, lemon and orange juice. When the redcurrant jelly has melted mix the sauce into the lamb and allow to stand for at least 30 minutes to marinate before serving.

In a saucepan, heat the oil and sauté the onion until slightly softened.

Add the rice and cook until the grains have changed from translucent to opaque. You need to stir the rice or it will catch on the base.

Add the stock, the mint and cinnamon stick, the shelled peas, carrots, salt and pepper.

Bring to the boil quickly and cover the pan. Turn the heat to low and cook gently until the rice has absorbed all the stock and the grains are tender. (It takes between 15 and 20 minutes.)

Remove and cool in a bowl, fluffing the rice with two forks. Remove the mint and cinnamon.

Place the rice on a platter. Level the top slightly and overlap the slices of lamb along the rice.

Most of the juice from the marinade will have been absorbed into the lamb; any left over can be spooned over the top. Decorate with some fresh mint sprigs.

Mustard-topped Racks of Lamb (below)

Mustard-topped Racks of Lamb

Small racks of lamb, slightly undercooked, are among the sweetest of all meats, and because they stay very moist, are excellent cold.

Allow one rack per person, either 3 or 4 chops, depending on appetites. The racks are cut after cooking and then coated with a lightly-jellied mustard.

Ideally, the racks should weigh between 250 g (8 oz) each and at the most up to 375 g (12 oz). Larger pieces of lamb will not be nearly as good and are stronger in flavour.

There is a salad of potatoes and peas underneath the lamb, but if you prefer you could serve the meat with other combinations such as a rice salad or a plain potato salad.

It is most important to remove as much fat from the lamb as possible; cold lamb fat is not particularly pleasant.

Serves 4	500 g (1 lb) peas
4 baby racks of lamb	salt
salt and pepper	**2 teaspoons sugar**
$\frac{1}{3}$ **cup (2$\frac{1}{2}$ fl oz) mayonnaise**	**mint**
1 tablespoon French	
mustard	Dressing:
1 teaspoon, hot,	**3 tablespoons vegetable oil**
English-style mustard	**1 tablespoon white wine**
1 tablespoon lemon juice	**vinegar**
1 teaspoon gelatine	**1 tablespoon finely**
500 g (1 lb) small new	**chopped parsley**
potatoes	**salt and pepper**
1 tablespoon finely	**1 teaspoon finely chopped**
chopped white onion	**mint**

Season the lamb with a little salt and pepper and wrap a small strip of foil around each bone to prevent charring.

Place into a moderate oven, 180–190°C (350–375°F/Gas 4–5), and cook for about 25 minutes for rare lamb, slightly longer for larger racks.

When ready, remove and leave to cool; wrap tightly in foil and chill.

Once they are cold, you can coat the lamb but it is best done only about 4 to 5 hours before serving.

Trim all the fat from the racks, leaving just the meat. Cut into chops.

Mix together the mayonnaise, mustards and lemon juice.

Mix the gelatine with 2 tablespoons of water, stirring until all the gelatine is mixed in. Stand the bowl in a pan of hot water until the gelatine is clear and completely dissolved.

Since the mayonnaise will be cold, it is best to add the mayonnaise to the bowl of gelatine, so that it mixes more evenly. Once the mayonnaise has been added, place the bowl in a basin of cold water and leave to cool until it is slightly thick.

Pat the top of the meat dry. Using a teaspoon, spread a layer of mayonnaise over the meat. If it is still too thin, do one layer, refrigerate the chops then trickle over a little more. Leave to set in the refrigerator.

Cook the potatoes, in their skins; cool and peel. Cut into small dice. Mix with the onion.

Shell the peas and cook with some salt, sugar and a sprig of mint. When ready, drain and if not mixing into the salad place them into cold water so they won't wrinkle or lose their fresh look.

To make the dressing, mix all the ingredients and either whisk or shake in a jar until thick.

Although the flavour of the dressing should not be too strong, if you find that this amount of dressing is not sufficient to coat the potatoes, make up a little more and moisten them again before serving.

Mix the peas with the potatoes and dressing and stir to coat.

Place the potatoes and peas in a mound on a long platter. Arrange the chops, with the bones to the centre, over the mound. Decorate with a few sprigs of mint.

Mixed salad Vietnamese style

The appearance of many little family-run Vietnamese restaurants in Australia is due mainly to the influx of people who fled from their country, often under tragic circumstances and with little money but with a strong desire to work.

Because of this influx, some new spices and herbs can now be obtained. One particular ingredient, Vietnamese sauce, nuoc nam, replaces the soy sauce which is used in most other Oriental countries. It is made from anchovies and is quite salty.

Vietnamese food can be very spicy, but the amount of chilli can be varied to suit individual palates. It has some interesting flavours, and with the use of lettuce, cucumber and Vietnamese mint, which tastes a little like coriander or Chinese parsley, is very fresh tasting.

This salad is an adaptation of some of the salads I have tried, and in it chillies are used very sparingly. The proportion of meat is small compared to the vegetables but for a light meal is sufficient; however, you can use more if you wish.

The salad can be made in advance, although the cabbage will soften and some moisture will form, but it will still taste delicious.

If you prefer a crisper texture, have the ingredients ready in a bowl and add the dressing about an hour before serving.

At a Vietnamese dinner this type of dish would be eaten as an appetiser, scooped up into prawn crisps.

If you use it as a first course it will serve 8 to 10 people.

Serves 4

185 g (6 oz) pork fillet
250 g (8 oz) chicken breast (boneless)
375 g (12 oz) cooked prawns
1 medium-sized white onion
1 tablespoon white wine vinegar
1 cucumber
2 cups finely shredded Chinese cabbage, firmly packed
$\frac{1}{2}$ cup grated carrot
1 tablespoon oil
2 tablespoons raw peanuts
2 eggs

1 tablespoon water
salt and pepper
some additional oil, to cook the omelettes
Vietnamese mint leaves, to garnish

Dressing:
1 tablespoon Vietnamese sauce
2 tablespoons water
1 clove garlic, crushed
1 teaspoon finely chopped fresh chilli
2 teaspoons sugar
1 tablespoon lemon juice

Remove any fat from the outside of the pork fillet.

Boil some salted water in a saucepan that is large enough to take the fillet. Add the fillet, cover the pan and simmer gently until cooked. The cooking time will depend on the size and shape of the meat.

When the pork is cooked, add the chicken breast to the water and simmer, without boiling, for about 3 to 4 minutes or until cooked.

Remove the meats to a bowl, adding a few spoonfuls of liquid to cover both meats so they will remain moist.

When cold, cut the pork into thin slices and then each slice into strips.

Tear the chicken breast into fine, long shreds.

Shell the prawns and chop into chunky pieces.

Cut the onion into quarters and then into small, thin slices. Cover with the vinegar and allow to stand for 1 hour. Drain before using. Peel the cucumber, cut in half lengthwise and then into slices.

Mix the pork, chicken and prawns with the onion, cucumber, cabbage and carrot.

Mix all the dressing ingredients together and stir well. Taste to check the salt; it should be well seasoned but if not salty enough add a little more Vietnamese sauce; if too salty, add more water.

Stir the dressing through so that everything is coated evenly.

Heat the oil, fry the peanuts until golden. Drain. The peanuts can be cooked beforehand but if you want them to remain crunchy, add them to the salad near to serving time because they soften in the mixture.

Beat the eggs with the water and add salt and pepper.

Heat enough oil to barely coat the base of a frying pan. Add sufficient egg to form a thin layer. (If the pan is an average size 20 cm (8 inch) omelette pan, you will get 2 from this mixture.)

Cook the eggs over medium heat until set. Turn out onto a board. Allow the omelettes to cool then roll them up tightly and cut into shreds.

When ready to serve, pack the salad into a 23 cm (9 inch) cake tin. Press down lightly so it will keep its shape when turned out, but don't squash the ingredients.

Turn out onto a platter and scatter the egg pieces in a mound on top. Decorate with Vietnamese mint leaves, or ordinary mint.

Polish Sausage salad

'Polish sausage' is more a generic term than a specific type of sausage.

Commercial Polish sausage is usually made from minced pork but sometimes a mixture of meats is used. It is precooked but can be successfully reheated.

In this salad the sausage is warmed and tossed with dressing just before serving; it won't be hot, just tepid.

This dish requires a certain amount of preparation in the presentation but it is not complicated and much of it can be done beforehand.

Make the dressing in one large quantity and then use a portion to mix with the cabbage salad, another with the potato and then mix the rest with some pepper and herbs and combine it with the sausage.

The salad looks attractive on a large, old-fashioned meat platter, it has a rustic, hearty flavour and is equally good in cold weather or on warmer days.

Serves 4
Dressing:
1 cup (8 fl oz) peanut oil
3 tablespoons white wine vinegar
$\frac{1}{4}$ cup (2 fl oz) mayonnaise
salt and pepper

Cabbage:
3 cups finely shredded cabbage
$\frac{1}{2}$ cup grated carrot
1 small white onion, finely diced
salt and pepper

Potato Salad:
250 g (8 oz) new potatoes
2 green or red peppers (capsicums)
250 g (8 oz) tomatoes, peeled

Sausage:
375 g (12 oz) Polish sausage (or similar)
1 teaspoon green peppercorns, crushed
2 tablespoons finely chopped parsley
1 tablespoon chives

Dressing: It is best to make the dressing first so it will be ready to use as each part of the salad is prepared.

Whisk the oil and vinegar together, add the mayonnaise and season with salt and pepper.

Cabbage: Mix the cabbage with the carrot and onion. Season with salt and pepper and add ½ cup of the dressing. Stir well and leave to stand for at least an hour. If not moist enough, use a little more dressing.

Potato Salad: Place the potatoes, in their skins, into a pot of salted water. Cook until they are tender.

While the potatoes are cooking, cut the peppers in half and remove the seeds. Flatten the peppers gently with the palm of your hand to make it easier to grill them evenly. Place under the griller and cook until the skin has blistered and is dark brown. Remove and leave to cool so you can handle them easily.

Peel away the transparent skin. Don't worry if any tiny pieces remain. Dice the peppers.

When the potatoes are cool enough to handle, peel and slice them.

Cut the tomatoes into small dice, removing some of the seeds.

Mix the peppers with the potatoes and tomatoes, season and stir through ⅓ cup of the dressing.

Sausage: Place the sausage in water and cook over gentle heat for about 20 minutes. Remove and slit the skin, peeling it away. Cut the sausage into thin slices.

Mix the remaining dressing, the peppercorns, parsley and chives and add the sausage, stirring to coat.

To assemble the salad: Place a circle of cabbage on the outside of the platter.

Arrange potato salad inside this, leaving a space in the centre and heap the sausage in this cavity, mounding slightly.

Shredded omelette for Mixed salad Vietnamese style (left)

Pork salad with Water Chestnuts

As a rule, dishes with pork can be heavy and substantial but this gently cooked fillet of pork, very moist and cut wafer-thin, makes a light and fragrant salad.

There is some chilli in the dressing; a teaspoonful gives it a little bite without being too hot but since individual tastes vary, you can adjust this. If you don't wish to use or handle fresh chilli add a few drops of Tabasco.

Baby lemon leaves also give a refreshing taste, but they do need to be the smallest ones—the well-formed green leaf would be too tough. You will find that as new shoots form on the tree they are thin and tinged with brown; these are the leaves to pick.

If you don't possess a lemon tree in the garden, add about ¼ teaspoon finely grated rind; it is not the same but is the best substitute.

The salad can be served in a large bowl, either plain or lined with some lettuce, although this is more for the sake of appearance.

If you wish to serve another dish, rice is the best accompaniment.

Serves 4	Dressing:
500 g (1 lb) fillet of pork	**1 clove garlic, crushed**
1 cup (8 fl oz) water	**2 tablespoons lemon juice**
1 tablespoon soy sauce	**3 teaspoons sugar**
2 strips fresh ginger	**1 tablespoon Vietnamese**
1 tablespoon sugar	**fish sauce**
200 g (6½ oz) water	**1 tablespoon finely**
chestnuts	**chopped coriander**
¾ cup grated carrot	**1 teaspoon finely chopped**
150 g (5 oz) bean shoots	**fresh chilli**
1 tablespoon vegetable oil	**4 baby lemon leaves, very**
2 onions, cut in thin	**finely chopped**
half-circles	

Trim the fat from the pork fillet. Place the meat into a saucepan with the water, soy sauce, ginger and sugar. Bring to the boil, cover, and simmer gently until tender. (The liquid should be barely simmering around the meat.) Cooking time will depend on whether the fillets are large and thick or long and thin.

Leave to cool in the liquid.

Remove the pork and cut into very thin, round slices. Place into a bowl.

Cut the water chestnuts into thin circles and add, along with the carrot.

Nip the root end from the bean shoots. Place the bean shoots into a small basin, cover with boiling water and leave to stand for 1 minute. Drain them and add to the pork.

Heat the oil and fry the onions for a few minutes until they have softened slightly.

Remove and mix, with the dressing, into the salad, tossing gently. To make the dressing, mix all the ingredients together and stir well. (There will only be a small amount of dressing but it should be sufficient.)

Leave the salad to stand for at least 1 hour before serving. It can be covered and chilled if you wish to make it several hours ahead, but remove from the refrigerator about 1 hour before serving so it is not too cold.

Chicken and Coriander salad (page 94)

Mixed salad Vietnamese style (page 86)

Mushroom–Stuffed Quail salad (page 104)

To cook Chicken for salads

1 chicken weighing approximately 1.5 kg (3 lb)	1 small onion, cut in thick slices
salt	handful of parsley,
4 peppercorns	including a few stalks

Place the chicken, breast side down, into a saucepan. Add enough water to barely cover the chicken. Season with salt and add the peppercorns, onion and parsley.

Bring the water gently to the boil. Cover and simmer over very low heat until the chicken is quite tender.

There is no need to turn the chicken over; the back portion contains very little flesh and what there is will be cooked from the steam in the saucepan. The most important thing is not to let the water boil; it should be kept so low that the flesh cooks without becoming firm.

Test with the point of a knife and when cooked, transfer the chicken and the liquid to a basin and leave to cool, keeping the breast side down so it remains moist.

The liquid will form a jelly. When you want to use the chicken, first lift off the fat that will have solidified on the jelly, then stand the basin in a sink with some hot water and leave for about 20 minutes until the jelly has dissolved. Lift the chicken out, remove the skin and dice the flesh as required for the recipe.

Chicken and Pea salad

I receive so many requests for substituting either frozen or freeze dried peas for fresh peas that I sometimes wonder whether people ever bother to shell peas. But the sight of the mounds of peas in the market reassures me, for such a supply must surely mean that the demand still exists.

There are no substitutes for the fresh peas in this recipe and it is a dish to treasure for the time of year when the first springtime peas appear.

Nothing can compare with their melting sweetness and in this recipe they combine beautifully with the strips of ham and tender chicken breast.

The salad is eaten on its own, with perhaps a small bowl of new potatoes as an accompaniment.

Serves 4

Peas:	
750 g (1½ lb) peas	1 tablespoon lemon juice
1 teaspoon salt	1 tablespoon finely chopped parsley
1 tablespoon sugar	1 tablespoon finely chopped mint
8 spring onions (scallions), cut into chunky pieces	

Dressing:	Chicken:
4 tablespoons vegetable or olive oil	4 chicken breasts
salt and pepper	2 tablespoons oil
	1 tablespoon lemon juice
	60 g (2 oz) ham, cut into long strips

Shell the peas and put them into a saucepan with a few of the pea pods, salt, sugar and the spring onions. Cover with boiling water and cook, without a lid, until the peas are tender. Taste, to make sure.

While they are cooking, prepare the dressing so that the peas can be added while they are hot.

In a salad bowl, mix the oil, some salt and pepper, the lemon juice, parsley and mint, and stir with a fork.

Drain the peas and remove the pods. Put the peas into the dressing, turning them over so they are well coated.

Skin the chicken breasts and flatten them gently between some waxed paper. Cut into long strips.

Heat the oil and add the chicken strips. Turn the heat up to medium-hot and cook for just a few minutes, turning them over so they cook evenly.

Remove the chicken to a bowl, season with salt and pepper and the lemon juice and add the ham. Stir gently to mix, and then fold into the peas.

You could eat this almost at once but it does keep for a short time. However, for the best flavour it is best not to refrigerate it, so make it only a few hours ahead of time.

Waldorf Chicken salad

The Waldorf Salad combination of apples, walnuts and celery goes well with chicken, except that a little less apple is needed.

In some recipes, the apples are not peeled; this is all right if you are using red-skinned eating apples. I like the flavour of Granny Smith apples but since they can have a very firm skin, it is usually best to peel them.

If you already have some cooked chicken, it is a very quick and easy salad to make and can be kept for a short time but is nicest if eaten a couple of hours after it is made.

Serves 4

	Dressing:
3 cups cooked chicken, cut into bite-sized pieces	½ cup (4 fl oz) mayonnaise
1 cup finely diced celery	½ cup (4 fl oz) cream
2 small Granny Smith apples, or red eating apples	2 teaspoons dry, hot English-style mustard
1 tablespoon lemon juice	
⅓ cup walnut pieces	
1 small white onion, finely chopped	
1 butter or mignonette lettuce	

Chill the celery in iced water to crisp it.

Place the chicken into a bowl and add the celery.

Peel and core the apples and cut into small dice. Sprinkle with lemon juice and toss to coat so that they will not discolour.

Add the apple with the walnut pieces and onion.

Mix all the dressing ingredients together. Stir into the salad. Cover, and stir again before using.

Place the lettuce into a bowl so that it extends slightly up the sides. Spoon the salad into this. Decorate with a few fresh walnut halves or pieces if you wish.

Chicken and Walnut salad (page 92)

Chicken and Pea salad (page 90)

Chicken salad with Apricots (page 93)

Chicken and Walnut salad

Served as a main dish on its own this may not be sufficient, so a rice salad or a noodle salad could be served as an accompaniment.

Although best served warm, it can be left to stand for a short time, but place the chicken and walnuts on the lettuce just before serving.

Instead of walnuts some pecan nuts can be tossed in the oil when cooking the strips of chicken breast.

The crunchy texture of the nuts is a good contrast to the softness of the chicken.

Serves 4

4 chicken breasts, each weighing about 125 g (4 oz)
salt and pepper
2 white onions
2 tablespoons vegetable oil
45 g (1½ oz) large walnut pieces or halves
8 lettuce leaves, torn into small pieces

Dressing:

3 tablespoons vegetable oil
1 tablespoon walnut oil
1 teaspoon honey
1 tablespoon white wine vinegar or lemon juice

Skin the chicken breasts and flatten them between waxed paper, using a meat mallet or a rolling pin.

Cut the chicken breasts into long, thin strips and season with salt and pepper.

Heat the oil in a frying pan.

Cut the onions in half and then into thin slices and add to the oil, tossing them until they have softened slightly. Remove to a bowl but leave the oil in the pan.

Turn the heat up and add the chicken and nuts. Toss for a few minutes, until the chicken is cooked, but be careful not to overcook it or it will become too firm.

Mix the chicken and nuts into the onions.

Immediately stir in the dressing, which you can prepare well ahead by mixing all the ingredients together and whisking lightly.

Have ready the lettuce, arranged on individual plates. Spoon the chicken, nuts and onion onto the bed of lettuce, add a little dressing to each portion, and serve immediately.

Chicken salad with Lightly Curried Leek sauce

Sautéed leeks mixed with a little curry powder, cream and stock make a tasty, naturally jellied sauce which is used to coat the chicken in this salad.

The various curry powders differ greatly in flavour and degree of 'hotness', so be careful that the one you are using is not too hot nor the flavour so strong that it overwhelms the leek.

It is most important that you cook the chicken beforehand so that the stock used in the sauce can be cooled and skimmed of any fat, or the cold fat will taste unpleasant.

This chicken dish should not be kept too long in the refrigerator because the sauce loses its flavour, so if you intend serving it for dinner, prepare it in the afternoon, rather than in the morning. However, the chicken can be cooked the day before; just be sure to keep it well covered with stock.

Serves 4

1 × 1.5 kg (3 lb) cooked chicken

Sauce:
30 g (1 oz) butter
2 tablespoons vegetable oil
1 bunch leeks
1 medium-sized Granny Smith apple
3 teaspoons medium-hot curry powder
2 cups (16 fl oz) stock from the chicken
1 cup (8 fl oz) cream
salt to taste
1 mignonette or butter lettuce
watercress sprigs, to garnish

The chicken should be cooked first, either in the morning or the day before (see page 90).

Strain the cooking liquid, refrigerate it and when the fat solidifies, remove it. Leave the chicken in the stock and refrigerate until required.

Heat the butter and oil in a saucepan.

Wash the leeks well and cut into very thin slices. You can use a little of the green part, but not if it is too tough.

Cook the leeks, stirring occasionally, until they are just slightly softened.

Peel and core the apple and dice it small. Add to the leeks and cook, covered, until the mixture is quite tender.

Add the curry powder and fry for a minute or two.

Add the chicken stock and simmer, covered, for a further 15 minutes.

Purée the mixture, in either a moulin or a food processor.

Return it to the saucepan, add the cream and cook, uncovered, until it is thick enough to coat the back of a spoon. The sauce will be a dull chartreuse colour.

Leave the sauce in a basin to cool; cover the basin to prevent a skin forming on top.

It is best to coat the chicken while the sauce is tepid so that when it sets it has a more even appearance.

Cut the chicken into portions; if there is moisture or jelly on top, wipe them dry. Place on a platter or rack and spoon a little of the leek sauce over them.

You can coat the chicken several times; if the sauce is a bit thin, refrigerate for about 10 minutes to set it.

Refrigerate the coated chicken pieces for a short time to set the topping. Don't leave it too long. If it is very cold the texture is not so pleasant.

You can either leave the chicken pieces ungarnished or place a few small watercress leaves on top before the coating sets.

Arrange the lettuce on a large platter. Place the chicken portions on the lettuce and tuck watercress pieces between them.

Chicken and Corn salad

Although there are many more ingredients than just chicken and corn in this salad, these two flavours predominate.

The use of chicken, corn, peppers and cos lettuce suggests an American influence and it is a salad that is probably more pleasing to English palates than European, who mostly regard corn as being more suitable for feeding to hens or for making oil.

You could buy the sweet corn on the cob and cook it yourself, but unless it is in the shops soon after picking it can be too firm, in which case the tinned product is better.

Serves 4

1 × 1.5 kg (3 lb) chicken	**Dressing:**
1 onion, sliced	$\frac{1}{2}$ cup (4 fl oz) vegetable oil
salt and pepper	2 tablespoons white
2 tablespoons vegetable oil	vinegar
2 additional (white) onions,	salt and pepper
cut in thin rings	
125 g (4 oz) mushrooms,	**Topping:**
cut in half or quartered	$\frac{1}{3}$ cup ($2\frac{1}{2}$ fl oz) mayonnaise
1 clove garlic, crushed	$\frac{1}{3}$ cup ($2\frac{1}{2}$ fl oz) cream
2 green or red peppers	
(capsicums)	
1 × 440 g (1 lb) tin whole	
kernel corn	
1 cos lettuce	

Put the chicken in a pan and add sufficient water to cover three-quarters of the bird. Add the sliced onion, salt and pepper.

Simmer gently until the chicken is cooked. Leave to cool in the liquid.

Skin the chicken and cut the meat into chunky, bite-sized pieces. You should have approximately $3\frac{1}{2}$ to 4 cups of firmly packed chicken.

Place into a large bowl and add the dressing.

To make the dressing, whisk together all the ingredients until thick.

In a frying pan, heat the oil and add the onion rings. Sauté, stirring occasionally, for about 5 minutes or until the onion has softened slightly. Mix with the chicken.

Put the mushrooms into the same pan and cook over high heat for about 1 minute. They should be dry, so don't let any liquid accumulate around them. Remove from the heat, season and add the garlic. Stir, and mix into the chicken.

Cut the peppers in half and remove the seeds. Flatten them slightly and place under a griller until the skin is blistered and tinged with dark brown. Leave to cool. When you can handle them, peel away the skin and cut the peppers into small pieces. Add them to the chicken mixture.

Drain the corn well and add it to the chicken mixture. Mix well so that everything is coated with dressing.

If it is to be kept for more than a couple of hours, cover and refrigerate but remove from the refrigerator about 30 minutes before serving so the salad won't be too cold.

Line a bowl with sections of cos lettuce so that it protrudes above the rim slightly. Stir the salad to moisten again and spoon into the centre.

Spread the top with the mayonnaise and cream mixed together.

Chicken salad with Apricots

Originally believed to come from Persia and Armenia, fresh sun-ripened apricots have a rich texture and an assertive flavour.

Try to buy fruit that has not been picked too soon, for it will not have the same sweetness of taste as the apricot that has been gently warmed to ripeness by the sun.

For this salad, only a little is needed in combination with the chicken, and the same idea could be used mixing chicken and peach. Less would be needed—about 2 yellow peaches for the 3 cups of chicken.

Apricots have a limited season and although the salad can be made with tinned apricots, it is not as good because once the fruit has been cooked it is soft and a little too sweet.

Serves 4

1 large Granny Smith	5 medium-sized ripe
apple	apricots
1 tablespoon oil	2 tablespoons flaked
1 teaspoon curry powder	almonds
3 cups (12 oz) cooked	
chicken, cut in bite-sized	**Dressing:**
pieces	$\frac{1}{2}$ cup (4 fl oz) mayonnaise
1 cup finely diced celery	$\frac{1}{3}$ cup ($2\frac{1}{2}$ fl oz) sour cream
1 tablespoon finely	1 tablespoon lemon juice
chopped spring onions	salt and pepper to taste
(scallions)	

Peel and core the apple and cut it into small dice.

Heat the oil in a pan and add the apple. Cook, stirring occasionally, until the fruit has softened slightly. Add the curry powder and stir to coat the apple.

Place into a bowl with the chicken, celery, and spring onions.

Cut 4 of the apricots in half and then into wedges. These shouldn't be too large, so about 4 from each half would be the right size.

Add the apricots to the chicken mixture.

Mix together all the dressing ingredients. Stir the dressing into the chicken mixture. Place the almonds into a dry frying pan. Cook, shaking the pan occasionally, until they are golden in colour. Set aside.

Arrange the salad in a bowl and sprinkle the almonds over the top.

Cut the remaining apricot into thin wedges and place on top of the salad, to garnish.

Chicken and Mango

This salad has the velvety richness of mango sauce coating sections of diced chicken.

Served in the mango cases it looks interesting, and because of the softness of the sauce I serve a crisp julienne of vegetables on one side. I use carrot, cucumber and peppers but you could add some celery if you wish or change the combination to suit your own taste.

Varieties of mango differ, as does the sweetness of the fruit. The dish should not be too sweet or the salad could be cloying, so decide when you make the sauce whether to add some more lemon juice, tasting as you go.

Buy mangoes that are not too fibrous, if you can, although after it is sieved, the pulp will be smooth.

Serves 4

4 small to medium-sized mangoes, about 200 g (6$\frac{1}{2}$ oz) each
3 cups (12 oz) cooked chicken, diced in bite-sized pieces

Sauce:
2 tablespoons cream
2 tablespoons mayonnaise
1 teaspoon grated fresh green ginger
salt and pepper
mango purée
a little lemon juice if needed

Julienne of Vegetables:
1 medium-sized carrot
$\frac{1}{2}$ medium-sized cucumber
1 small green pepper (capsicum)
2 tablespoons vegetable oil
3 teaspoons white vinegar or lemon juice
reserved mango sauce

Cut the mangoes in half, working the knife around the stone. Carefully lift off the two halves and keep them intact to form the cases.

Scrape out the mango flesh. Push it through a sieve and leave the pulp in a bowl for the sauce.

Chill the mango shells.

To make the sauce, mix the cream, mayonnaise, ginger, a little salt and pepper with the mango purée and then add lemon juice if necessary.

Reserve $\frac{1}{4}$ cup of this sauce for the julienne of vegetables. Mix the remainder of the sauce with the diced chicken and fill the mango cases. Keep them chilled. (They can be prepared several hours beforehand.)

Peel the carrot, cut into long, very thin slices and then across into small strips about the size of a matchstick.

Peel the cucumber, cut into quarters, lengthwise. Remove the seeds and cut the cucumber into long strips.

Cut the pepper in half. Remove the seeds and slice the pepper into long, fine shreds.

Place the vegetables into iced water for about 30 minutes to crisp them.

Whisk the oil with the vinegar or lemon juice and the reserved mango sauce.

Drain the vegetables and pat them completely dry with some kitchen paper.

Place into a bowl and add the sauce, stirring to coat them lightly.

Serves 2 small mango cases per person and place a little pile of the vegetables alongside. If small mangoes are not available, serve half a large one per person.

Pineapple and Chicken salad

For this dish, choose small pineapples so that each person can be served an individual half. Make sure that the tops are green and undamaged and do not have brown spikes on them.

If you can't buy the right size, choose a large pineapple and spoon out the servings from the shell onto individual plates.

Serves 4

2 small pineapples
3 cups (12 oz) cooked chicken, cut into bite-sized pieces
1 teaspoon oil
45 g (1$\frac{1}{2}$ oz) blanched almonds, cut in half
1 teaspoon curry powder
3 tablespoons desiccated coconut, to garnish

Dressing:
3 tablespoons vegetable oil
1 tablespoon white wine vinegar
2 tablespoons juice from the pineapple
2 tablespoons cream
2 tablespoons mayonnaise
salt and pepper

Cut the pineapple in half lengthwise, cutting through the tops carefully so the halves will be even.

Using either a grapefruit knife or a small sharp knife, carefully cut the flesh from the shell. Remove the core and dice the remainder. You will need only 1$\frac{1}{2}$ cups of diced pineapple for the salad so the remaining flesh can be kept aside for another use.

Turn the pineapple shells upside down until you are ready to use them. This will drain away any liquid that collects and will prevent them from becoming soggy. Reserve 2 tablespoons of the drained pineapple juice for the sauce.

Mix the pineapple with the chicken.

Heat the oil in a small frying pan, add the almonds and cook them over a medium heat, stirring lightly until they are toasted and golden.

Add the curry powder and stir so it coats the almonds. Mix the almonds into the pineapple and chicken.

Toast the coconut in a dry pan until golden, remove and keep aside to garnish the salad.

To make the dressing, whisk the oil and vinegar together, add the pineapple juice and then stir in the cream and mayonnaise. Season with salt and pepper.

Stir the dressing through the pineapple and chicken mixture.

When ready to serve, spoon the mixture into the shells and sprinkle with a little of the toasted coconut.

Chicken and Coriander salad

It is not only the aroma and taste of coriander, or Chinese parsley as it is sometimes known, that gives this salad an Oriental flavour, but the crispy bean shoots, snow peas and sesame seeds in combination with roasted chicken. However, if you think there may be too much coriander in it for your taste, add just a little at first and then increase it if you like.

The salad needs nothing else with it because it has sufficient variety to be served as a complete meal.

Serves 4

1 × 1.5 kg (3 lb) chicken
salt and pepper
1 tablespoon vegetable oil
30 g (1 oz) butter
$\frac{1}{3}$ cup spring onions
(scallions), cut into
chunky pieces
2 tablespoons sesame seeds
2 tablespoons finely
chopped fresh coriander
(Chinese parsley)
125 g (4 oz) snow peas
90 g (3 oz) bean shoots
12 lettuce leaves

Dressing:
$\frac{3}{4}$ cup (6 fl oz) vegetable oil
1 tablespoon soy sauce
2 tablespoons lemon juice
3 teaspoons sugar

Season the chicken with salt and pepper. Rub the outside with the oil and place the butter over the breast.

Bake in a moderate oven, 190°C (375°F/Gas 5), for about 1 hour, or until cooked and golden on the outside. Don't overcook the chicken; it will continue to cook a little as it cools.

Remove from the oven, cover lightly with foil and leave to cool completely.

Remove all the meat from the bones, discard the skin if you wish, although since it will be well-flavoured it could be used.

Cut the meat into chunky but large bite-sized pieces. Mix with the spring onions.

Place the sesame seeds into a dry frying pan. Cook over a medium heat, shaking the pan occasionally, until the seeds are toasted and golden.

Add the seeds to the chicken, together with the coriander.

Using a fork or whisk, mix the dressing ingredients together until thick. Divide in half. To one half add 2 teaspoons hot Chinese mustard; leave the other half plain.

Mix the chicken with the half quantity of dressing that contains the hot mustard.

Cover and leave to stand for about 30 minutes. It is better not to refrigerate the chicken because it tends to dry out. If you need to, cover well, and remove 30 minutes before serving.

Trim the ends and string the snow peas. Cook them in boiling salted water for about a minute, or until bright green.

Drain and run cold water over them so they stop cooking and retain their colour.

Pinch away the root end of the bean shoots.

Toss the snow peas and bean shoots together, but don't add the dressing until just before serving the salad or they will soften.

To assemble the salad, make a bed of lettuce on the base of a large platter. Mix the other half of the dressing with the snow peas and bean shoots and arrange them in a nest shape around the edge of the platter. Stir the chicken well and mound it in the centre of the vegetables. Serve at once.

Chicken salad in Cantaloupe Shells

A very light and delicate salad, it is perfect for summer lunch.

Early in the season you can buy tiny canteloupes; these look most attractive with the salad heaped into the shell.

If you cannot obtain the small canteloupes, buy a larger melon, fill it with the salad and spoon it into the lettuce cups at the table.

Serves 4

4 cups chicken, cut into
bite-sized pieces
2 small canteloupes
(melon)

Dressing:
1 egg
$\frac{1}{2}$ teaspoon salt
white pepper
1 cup (8 fl oz) vegetable oil
2 teaspoons grated fresh
ginger

2 tablespoons lemon juice
1 tablespoon finely
chopped ginger in syrup

Garnish:
2 tablespoons flaked
almonds
1 tablespoon finely
chopped glacé ginger
lettuce leaves

Cut the canteloupes in half and remove the seeds.

Using a melon baller, scoop out small balls of the melon. You will need about 8 per person. (You will probably find there is more canteloupe than you need; any left over can be used in a fruit salad.)

Scrape the shells clean and chill them.

The dressing, a light mayonnaise, can be made either by hand or in a food processor.

To make the dressing, beat the egg with salt and pepper. Gradually add the oil, a little at a time, whisking or beating well until you have added about three-quarters. Add the lemon and then the rest of the oil. Lastly, mix in the chopped ginger. Cover and chill if not using immediately.

Mix the canteloupe and chicken with $\frac{3}{4}$ cup of the dressing. Cover and chill for at least 1 hour.

Spoon the mixture into the shells.

Toast the almond flakes lightly by heating in a dry pan until golden. (You can do this well beforehand.)

Coat the mixture in the shells with a thin layer of mayonnaise and garnish with some almond flakes and a little glacé ginger. Serve immediately.

Chicken in Tarragon cream

It is believed that tarragon originally came from Siberia, although we associate it mainly with European cooking, in which some of the most important sauces need this herb for their base.

Aromatic yet delicate in flavour, French tarragon is more difficult to grow than the Russian variety but far superior in taste.

Tarragon has a wonderful affinity with chicken, provided not too much is used. A number of great 'starred' restaurants throughout Europe specialise in Chicken with Tarragon Sauce, the portions arriving bathed in a perfumed sauce, almost tinged a pale green shade from the leaves of the herb.

A cold tarragon sauce served with chicken is equally successful. When the chicken stock is reduced and mixed with cream it will jell sufficiently to coat the chicken and set without needing any added gelatine. This coating for the chicken makes a light layer to coat the top. If you want a more generous layer of sauce, double the quantity exactly.

The sauce needs to be made with French tarragon; a generous sprig which is at least as long as your hand will flavour the sauce perfectly.

Because of the delicate flavour of this dish, rice or potatoes are the best accompaniments.

Serves 4
1 × 1.5 kg (3 lb) chicken
1 onion, sliced
salt and white pepper
1 generous large sprig fresh tarragon

$\frac{3}{4}$ cup (6 fl oz) thick cream
an additional, large piece fresh tarragon
mignonette lettuce
tarragon leaves, to garnish

Place the chicken into a saucepan, breast side down, and add sufficient water to cover at least three-quarters of the bird.

Add the onion, some salt, white pepper and one sprig of fresh tarragon.

Simmer very gently, covered, until the chicken is quite tender. You can turn it over if you wish, although there is almost no meat on the back of the chicken and it is more important to keep the breast covered all the time so that it stays moist.

Leave to cool, placed in a bowl, breast side down and surrounded by the liquid. When cold, remove all traces of fat from the top of the stock, which will jell or become slightly firm when refrigerated. To dissolve the jelly, warm the bowl gently so the chicken can be easily removed.

Cut the chicken into portions, removing the legs, wings and breast, and discard the skin.

Place $1\frac{1}{2}$ cups of stock from the chicken into a pan, add the cream and the additional sprig of tarragon.

Cook the stock, uncovered, until it has reduced by about half.

Leave to cool and remove the piece of tarragon. Check the seasoning and if adding pepper make sure it is white.

Place the chicken on a plate and spoon a little of the sauce over the top of each piece to coat it.

Place into the refrigerator but leave the remainder of the sauce at room temperature so that it won't set.

After about 10 minutes the chicken should be coated with a fine film of sauce which has become firm. Coat again with the sauce several times, letting each coat set before you apply the next.

If a lot of the mixture has run onto the plate and you need extra, remove it with a spatula, melt it, and use it again.

Keep the chicken chilled until serving time, but don't let it become too firm. The preparation should be done about 5 hours before the meal.

Decorate each portion of chicken with fresh tarragon leaves.

Spread a layer of lettuce on a platter and arrange the chicken portions on it.

Chinese Chicken salad with Fried Noodles

This chicken salad is covered with crisp, puffy noodles. It may look light but is quite a filling dish.

If you would prefer to serve it as a first-course, the same quantity serves 8.

Serves 4
4 chicken breasts
chicken stock or water
salt and pepper
1 thick slice of fresh green ginger
6 spring onions (scallions), roughly chopped
$\frac{1}{2}$ cup (2 oz) cashew nuts
10 lettuce leaves, shredded very finely
cooking oil

60 g (2 oz) Chinese rice noodles

Dressing:
1 teaspoon hot Chinese mustard
pinch 5 spice powder
2 tablespoons soy sauce
2 teaspoons sesame oil
1 tablespoon vegetable oil
2 teaspoons lemon juice
1 teaspoon sugar

Heat the stock or water in a pan, season with salt and pepper, if necessary, and add the strip of ginger.

Remove and discard the skin from the chicken breasts and add them to the liquid. Cover the pan and have the liquid barely simmering. The chicken must not be boiled or it will become too firm. Unless the chicken pieces are very large, about 5 to 6 minutes should be long enough.

Remove to a bowl and place a little of the liquid over the top to keep them moist while they cool.

Make up the dressing by mixing all the ingredients together in a bowl.

Cut the chicken into small, thin strips. Cover with the dressing, adding the spring onions and nuts.

Make a bed of shredded lettuce on a flat, oval platter.

Heat sufficient oil to fry the noodles; it must be so hot that they puff almost instantly when added. It is best to do just a few at a time; they will be very crisp and light. If the oil is not hot enough, the noodles will be tough and have a most unpleasant texture.

Place the chicken on the lettuce and scatter the noodles over the top to cover completely. Serve immediately.

Chicken Oriental

I have some reservations as to whether this name is really appropriate since the salad combines both Chinese and western ingredients.

However, the name was given by a friend of mine who finds this salad invaluable to keep in the refrigerator for a quick weekend meal as a simple dish followed by some cheese and fruit to serve for unexpected guests.

It has an advantage over some of the chicken salads in that it does seem to refrigerate quite well without losing flavour and becoming too firm, but be sure not to overcook the chicken breast.

Accompany with some rice on the side, if you wish.

Serves 4

500 g (1 lb) chicken breast (fillets)
salt and pepper
2 tablespoons vegetable oil
1 tablespoon white wine vinegar
1 tablespoon soy sauce
3 additional tablespoons vegetable oil
1 tablespoon finely
chopped glacé ginger
1 small cucumber
100 g (3½ oz) small white mushrooms
½ cup grated carrot

Garnish:
2 tablespoons finely chopped spring onions (scallions) or chives
lettuce leaves

Flatten the chicken breasts slightly and season with salt and pepper. Cut into strips approximately 5 cm × 1 cm (2 inches × ½ inch).

Heat the oil in a frying pan. Sauté the chicken strips, turning them frequently so they cook evenly. Don't overcook them, just a few minutes should be sufficient.

Remove from the heat, but make the sauce immediately as it should be placed over the chicken while it is warm.

Mix together the vinegar, soy sauce, 3 tablespoons oil and the ginger. Pour into the pan over the chicken strips. Return the pan to the heat and warm the chicken again for a minute. Put into a bowl and leave to cool.

Using a vegetable peeler, peel off strips of skin from the cucumber, leaving some on for colour.

Cut the cucumber in half lengthwise and then into wafer-thin slices.

Cut the mushrooms into very thin slices, removing the stalks if tough.

Add the cucumber, mushrooms and grated carrot to the chicken and stir well.

Leave to marinate for at least 1 hour. If keeping longer, cover tightly and refrigerate.

When serving, spoon onto lettuce and scatter either spring onions or chives on top.

Chinese Chicken salad with Fried Noodles (page 96)
Chicken Oriental (above)

Duck and Pickled Ginger salad (page 103)

Chicken in Tarragon cream (page 96)

Chicken and Mango (page 94)

Chicken in Curried cream

Curried chicken salad is an all-time favourite and this is one of the nicest. The quantities can easily be doubled or trebled for larger servings.

It keeps quite well refrigerated for a short time. The sauce can be made and the chicken cooked on the previous day.

It is good with the type of accompaniments you would serve with any hot curried dish, such as rice and cucumber salad, and can be garnished with fruit.

Serves 4

1 × 1.5 kg (3 lb) cooked chicken
2 tablespoons vegetable oil
1 medium-sized white onion, finely chopped
2 teaspoons curry powder
1 tablespoon tomato sauce (ketchup)
2 teaspoons apricot jam
2 teaspoons paw paw and mango chutney
$\frac{1}{4}$ cup (2 fl oz) oil mayonnaise
$\frac{1}{4}$ cup (2 fl oz) cream
mango or paw paw (papaya), to garnish

Skin the chicken and divide into portions; remove the bones, if you wish.

Heat the oil and add the onion. Sauté, stirring occasionally, until quite soft. Add the curry powder and fry for 1 minute.

Remove the pan from the heat, then add the tomato sauce and jam. If the jam is lumpy, chop up the pieces.

Add chutney and leave to cool.

Mix into the mayonnaise.

Whip the cream until it holds soft peaks and add it to the mayonnaise. (If the mayonnaise is very thick you may barely have to whip the cream as it is best if the mayonnaise is not too heavy and thick.)

Place the chicken pieces on a platter and coat with sauce so all the flesh is covered.

Chill until serving time. Don't leave it too long, although you can prepare it in the morning if serving at dinner time.

You will need only $\frac{1}{2}$ a large mango or 1 small one for garnish, or the same of paw paw. Peel and cut into thin slices. Arrange these either in a circle on top, or around the edge of the chicken.

Chicken and Egg Noodle salad

Combined with coriander, ginger, sesame oil and thin noodles, this chicken salad is very light and aromatic.

Serve it in a large bowl. You could place some young lettuce leaves on the base, if you wish, but more for appearance than taste because it needs nothing else beyond the flavourings here.

Serves 4

1 × 1.5 kg (3 lb) chicken
1 cup (8 fl oz) dry white wine
2 strips fresh ginger
1 teaspoon salt
1 cucumber, approximately 375 g (12 oz)
$\frac{1}{3}$ cup chopped spring onions
250 g (8 oz) fine egg noodles
250 g (8 oz) ham, cut in thin strips

Dressing:

$\frac{1}{3}$ cup (2$\frac{1}{2}$ fl oz) stock, from cooking the chicken
1 teaspoon dry, English-style mustard
1 tablespoon sesame oil
1 tablespoon vegetable oil
3 tablespoons soy sauce
1 clove garlic, crushed
2 teaspoons sugar
1 teaspoon ground ginger
1 tablespoon ground coriander

Place the chicken into a saucepan, breast side down, and add enough water to cover three-quarters of the bird. Add white wine, ginger and salt. Bring to the boil, cover and simmer over low heat until tender, turning it over once. Leave to cool in the liquid, making sure that the chicken has the breast covered while cooling so it keeps moist.

Peel the cucumber, cut in half lengthwise and remove the seeds with a teaspoon. Cut into very thin slices and place in a bowl. Sprinkle with a little salt and sugar.

Leave to stand for 30 minutes or longer. Drain the cucumber and squeeze out the liquid.

Soak the noodles in water for 10 minutes, then cook in a pot of salted boiling water.

While the noodles are cooking make up the dressing by mixing all the ingredients in a bowl.

Drain the noodles and mix with the dressing while they are hot.

Remove the chicken from the liquid. Peel away the skin and cut the chicken into small pieces.

Add the meat to the noodles with the cucumber and ham and toss well.

This salad is best if not chilled but if you do have to make it ahead of time, cover tightly and chill. Remove from the refrigerator about an hour before serving and toss lightly to separate if it has become packed down in the bowl.

Chicken and Egg Noodle salad

Chicken in Curried cream

Duck salad with Lemon

An exotic yet light, fresh dish of duck pieces marinated in a lemon and ginger sauce. This is topped with lightly fried, crunchy curls of duck skin.

It needs little else, except perhaps some potato or, even better, a plain rice dish to accompany it.

Cook the duck on the day it is to be eaten to ensure that it is moist and fresh. Once refrigerated, it will become firm and will not absorb the marinade as well.

Serves 4
1 × 2 kg (4 lb) duckling
fresh thyme
3 slices lemon
1 teaspoon fresh ginger,
  grated into shreds
salt

Dressing:
½ cup (4 fl oz) water or
  chicken stock
2 teaspoons grated fresh
  green ginger
1 tablespoon soy sauce

2 tablespoons sugar
⅓ cup (2½ fl oz) lemon juice

Salad:
1 large cucumber
salt
1 teaspoon sugar
1 tablespoon lemon juice
1 cup celery, cut into thin
  slices
lettuce leaves
about 18 small sprigs
  watercress
12 spring onions (scallions)

Place the thyme, lemon and shredded ginger into the body cavity of the duck. Truss the legs and rub some salt on the outside of the bird. Prick the skin well.

Place into a baking dish and cook in a moderate oven, 180°C (350°F/Gas 4), pricking the skin several times and turning the duck over as it cooks. Cook until tender. The skin should be crisp and a deep golden colour and most of the duck fat will have been released. Remove and leave until cool enough to handle.

Meanwhile make the dressing: Place all the ingredients into a small saucepan. Boil rapidly until reduced by half.

You can prepare the dressing several hours ahead, just warm it again before using to marinate the duck pieces. As the mixture cools, it will flavour the meat.

Remove all the skin from the duck and cut the meat into bite-sized pieces.

Pour some of the dressing over the meat and leave to marinate for at least 1 hour.

Cut the duck skin into long, thin strips. Place them into a frying pan that has just sufficient vegetable oil to coat the base.

Cook over fairly high heat, turning the pieces of skin over once. The strips will curl and become very crisp. Drain them on kitchen paper; they will remain crisp for several hours.

Salad: Peel the cucumber, score the outside with a fork. Cut the cucumber into wafer-thin slices and place into a bowl with salt, sugar and lemon juice. Let it stand for 30 minutes and then drain. Squeeze firmly.

Place the celery into iced water and leave to become very crisp.

Break the lettuce into small pieces and refrigerate with the watercress.

Trim the spring onions so that just a little of the green portion remains. Using a sharp knife, finely slash the green part half-way up towards the white end, like a fringe. Place in iced water so the ends will curl and ruffle out.

To assemble the salad cover the base of a platter with lettuce pieces. Form a ring of cucumber around the edge and place the drained, crisp celery in the centre. Spoon the duck and its sauce over the celery. Scatter some watercress sprigs and spring onions around the edge and place crisp duck skin on top of the duck, once assembled, serve as soon as possible or the lettuce will become soggy.

Duck salad with Cherries and Orange

Melbourne Cup Day, which falls on the first Tuesday in November, is distinguished not only by the famous horse race but by the fact that, in Melbourne, regardless of the weather conditions, the season's first cherries always make their appearance at the markets.

A fruit to be treasured because of its short season, cherries can be used in both a sweet or sour guise, depending on the variety.

Fresh cherries are used in this recipe; I prefer the sweet ones but this is a matter of taste.

If cherries are not in season, the dish could be made with the tinned product, but drain them well.

The salad is quite simple to prepare, and along with the cherries and orange has just the slightest trace of mint coating the meat.

It makes a substantial meal, with perhaps only a simple potato dish or some rice, if you feel it needs an accompaniment.

Serves 4
1 × 2 kg (4 lb) duck
½ orange, cut in quarters
generous sprig parsley
generous sprig thyme
generous sprig sweet savory
salt and pepper

Salad:
1 cup finely diced celery
250 g (8 oz) fresh cherries,
  or well-drained tinned
  cherries
¼ cup (2 fl oz) orange juice

2 teaspoons sugar
3 oranges
1 butter lettuce

Dressing:
cooking liquid from the
  cherries
1 scant tablespoon
  redcurrant jelly
1 tablespoon finely
  chopped mint
½ cup (4 fl oz) vegetable oil
2 tablespoons lemon juice
salt and pepper

Wash and dry the duck and place the orange and herbs in the body cavity. Season well with salt and pepper and prick the skin over the breast and legs.

Bake in a moderate oven, 180°C (350°F/Gas 4). Prick the skin several times during cooking to release the fat. When cooked, the skin should be crisp and the juices of the duck run clear when pricked.

Remove and leave to cool until you can handle the bird. Remove all the flesh and cut into bite-sized pieces. You can use the skin or remove it, but if not too fatty it is delicious.

Salad: Place the celery into iced water to crisp.

Remove the stones from the cherries. Place the cherries into a small saucepan with the orange juice and sugar and bring to the boil. Place a lid on the pan and cook over very low heat for about 5 minutes or until just slightly softened.

Remove and drain, but keep the liquid to use in the dressing.

Peel and remove the outside white pith from the orange. Cut out the orange segments and mix with the cherries.

Add the cherries and celery to the duck.

Mix through the dressing (see below) and leave to stand for about 1 hour for the flavours to blend. You can leave it much longer if you wish, but the celery will soften slightly. If you prefer the celery crisp, add it nearer to serving time.

Dressing: Place the first three ingredients into a small saucepan and warm gently until the jelly has dissolved. Pour into a bowl and mix in the oil and lemon juice. Add the salt and pepper. You don't need to let this cool; you can add it to the duck immediately it is made.

To assemble, arrange the butter lettuce around the edge of a platter. Stir the duck mixture and place it down the centre of the lettuce. If you feel there is too much liquid in the duck, leave some aside.

Serve as soon as possible or the lettuce will become soggy.

Duck and Pickled Ginger salad

This is quite a spectacular salad, both in appearance and taste.

It requires some preparation beforehand as the ginger pickle needs to stand for 24 hours before being used.

The fresh ginger must be peeled and then cut wafer-thin so it will give the right flavour, without too much heat.

Rambutans, close relatives of the lychee and native to Malaysia, are mixed with the duck. Fresh rambutans are covered with red, or sometimes yellow spikes, and are slightly firmer in texture than lychees. You can buy them in tins. If they are not obtainable, use tinned lychees.

I cut the rambutans in half lengthwise as they are quite large but lychees could be left whole.

If you feel a side salad is needed, serve a very simple rice dish.

Serves 4

Pickled Ginger:
**24 wafer-thin slices of
  peeled, fresh ginger
table salt
1 tablespoon sugar
1 tablespoon white vinegar**

Dressing:
**2 tablespoons soy sauce
1 tablespoon vegetable oil
2 teaspoons sesame oil
1 tablespoon lemon juice
2 teaspoons hoi sin sauce
liquid from the pickled
  ginger**

Salad:
**1 × 1.75 g (3½ lb) duck
salt and pepper
1 chunky piece fresh green
  ginger, about the size of a
  walnut
2 red peppers (capsicums)
1 × 450 g (1 lb) tin seedless
  rambutans
2 Chinese gooseberries
  (kiwi fruit)
1 lettuce (either mignonette
  or butter lettuce)**

Pickled Ginger: Place the ginger on a flat plate and sprinkle with salt. Leave to stand for several hours. The ginger will look slightly wet at the end of this time. Rinse in a sieve and shake dry.

Place the ginger into a small bowl and stir in the sugar and vinegar. Leave to stand for 24 hours before using. Drain, and reserve the liquid for the dressing.

Dressing: Mix all the ingredients together; if not fresh tasting, add a little more lemon juice. It shouldn't need any salt or pepper; the soy sauce will provide salt and the pickled ginger liquid the spice.

Salad: Season the duck inside and out with salt and pepper. Place the ginger inside the cavity and prick the skin of the duck well, especially over the breast.

Place the duck into a lightly-oiled baking tin and cook in a moderate oven, 180°C (350°F/Gas 4). Turn the duck as it cooks and prick the skin several times to release the fat. If you find that a lot of fat is accumulating, drain some of it away.

Test to see if the bird is cooked by pricking the skin near the leg. When the juices run clear, remove from the oven. Don't overcook the duck; it will continue to cook as it cools but be sure it isn't firm or the flesh will become dry when served cold. The skin should be a golden colour and quite crisp.

Leave the duck to cool and when cold remove all the flesh and cut it into bite-sized pieces. Whether or not you remove the skin is optional; if it is not too fatty and a little crisp it is delicious.

Mix the duck with the dressing and add the pickled ginger, stirring well.

Cut the peppers in half and remove the seeds. Place under a preheated griller and cook until the skin is blistered and a dark colour. Remove, and when cool enough to handle, carefully peel away the papery skin. Cut the pepper into tiny pieces.

Drain the rambutans and cut each one in half lengthwise.

Mix the peppers and fruit into the duck and leave to stand several hours. If leaving longer, cover tightly and refrigerate.

Peel the Chinese gooseberries and slice them ready for the garnish.

Cover the base of an oval platter with lettuce. Stir the salad to mix through any dressing that may have accumulated on the base and spoon it onto the lettuce. Arrange a line of Chinese gooseberries along the top.

Warm Quail salad

A beautiful salad, in the tradition of the new and more unusual salads which have become popular in Europe, this is often served as a first course.

One quail, lightly cooked and sitting on lettuce makes a very good first course for a special dinner. Two quail, accompanied by some fresh crusty bread, are sufficient for a main dish.

Some of the cooking is done at the last minute and requires undivided attention for the few minutes it takes to reheat the quail and assemble the salad.

There is a certain amount of preparation required but most of it can be done ahead of time. Then, if the dressing is ready, and the lettuce, watercress and eggs are arranged on the plates, you have only to concentrate on the actual cooking.

The quail are cooked and then cut into portions. Whole quail presented on lettuce would be very unmanageable for the diner.

Although the quail are reheated, they will be only barely warm by the time the dish is served. They are at their best then, juicy and with the full flavour of the bird freshened with lettuce and cress.

With this type of dish you can serve a substantial first course, such as some crêpes, a piece of fish or a soup.

Serves 4	Dressing:
8 quail	6 tablespoons light olive oil
8 sprigs thyme	2 tablespoons white wine
salt and pepper	vinegar
vegetable oil	1 tablespoon finely
250 g (8 oz) small button	chopped fresh chervil
mushrooms	1 tablespoon finely
16 quail eggs	chopped parsley
butter lettuce	salt and pepper
watercress sprigs	

Wash and dry the quail and place a sprig of thyme in the body cavity of each one. Season with salt and pepper. Brush the outside of each bird with a little oil and tie the legs together.

Place into a small dish and bake in a moderate oven, 180°–190°C (350°–375°F/Gas 4–5), for about 15 minutes, or until the outside of the quail is a light colour and the breast meat is almost cooked. (They will be cooked again later so must be pink at this stage.)

Remove and leave to cool slightly so you can handle the birds easily.

Cut the legs away and then carefully remove each breast. Place on a plate but keep the portions separate because, later, the legs will be reheated before the breasts.

Cut the stalks of the mushrooms level with the caps. Wipe the tops with some kitchen paper and set aside.

Cook the quail eggs for about 3 to 4 minutes and shell them. Cut each one in half lengthwise and cover tightly. Store in the refrigerator.

Prepare the dressing: mix the oil and vinegar with the fresh chervil, if you can obtain some, and the parsley. Season lightly with salt and pepper. Set aside.

Arrange the lettuce on individual plates and place sprigs of watercress around the edge. Place the quail egg halves on the cress.

To cook the quail and mushrooms, you will need two frying pans. Heat a little oil to barely coat the base of one pan. Add the quail legs and cook over fairly high heat, turning them once, until cooked through and hot. They should take about 3 minutes.

While they are cooking, heat a little oil in the second pan and add the mushrooms and seasoning. Cook for only a couple of minutes. Remove from the heat.

Push the quail legs to one side of the first pan, add the breasts and cook for about 1 minute.

Place the breasts in the centre of the lettuce with the mushrooms alongside. Arrange the quail legs on top of the mushrooms.

Pour the dressing into the pan in which the quail was cooked and stir it around. Spoon a little over the top of each salad. Serve as soon as you can.

Mushroom-stuffed Quail salad

This salad comprises quail which are filled with a flavoursome mushroom stuffing and are served with a nest of quail eggs. It looks beautiful but, since it does involve some time in the preparation, it is a special occasion dish. Ideally the quail should be boned. This is really no different from boning a chicken, but of course more awkward because of the tiny bones.

Cut down the back of the quail and then carefully pull away some of the skin and expose the wing joint. Cut this at the joint— both wings and legs are left on the quail—only the rib cage is removed. Cut down one side of the rib cage, cut through the joint of the leg and then repeat on the other side. At first it is slow but actually it is not too difficult to do despite the smallness of the birds. You can bone quail before preparing this dish and freeze them most successfully.

If you don't wish to tackle this, stuff the quail unboned, using the same stuffing but being sure to pack it tightly to get as much inside the cavity as possible.

It is best to cook the quail only a few hours before serving if possible, so they are cool but not too cold. Once refrigerated, they become firm and are not quite as tasty. It is a light meal, accompanied by a nest made from alfalfa and carrot and garnished with quail eggs. Of course you can serve other salads with it. Potato salad or a rice salad are good.

Serves 4	1 large egg
8 quail	oil for cooking the quail
45 g (1½ oz) butter	mignonette or baby lettuce
1 tablespoon vegetable oil	leaves
1 small onion, finely	2 small mushrooms to
chopped	garnish
1 clove garlic, finely	alfalfa
chopped	⅓ cup finely grated carrot,
375 g (12 oz) mushrooms	firmly packed
½ cup (4 fl oz) dry white	lemon juice
wine	12 quail eggs, hard-boiled
1 teaspoon Worcestershire	and shelled
sauce	violets
salt and pepper	
½ cup (1 oz) breadcrumbs,	
made from stale bread	

Wash the quail and pat dry. Bone them if you wish, leaving in the legs and wings. Melt the butter in a pan, add the onion and garlic and sauté gently until they have softened and are a very pale golden colour. Stir occasionally.

Remove the stems from the mushrooms if they are woody and chop the mushrooms into very fine dice. Add them to the pan and cook until they are tender, keeping the heat fairly high so that the mixture won't stew and become too wet. Add the wine and boil rapidly until it has completely evaporated.

Place the mixture into a bowl, adding the Worcestershire sauce, salt and pepper. Leave to cool slightly then add the breadcrumbs and egg.

Fill the centre cavity of the quail with this mixture. If they have been boned you will need to sew them up, if not the filling will stay inside quite well provided it is firmly packed. Tie the legs together with string and brush the quail with oil.

Place them on a rack in a baking dish and bake in a preheated oven 180°C (350°F/Gas 4) for about 20 minutes, turning once. The quail should not be overcooked as they continue cooking a little even when removed from the oven. Wrap them in foil and leave to cool. Brush the breast with a little vegetable oil to keep them shiny before serving. Cut the additional mushrooms into very thin slices. Place a couple on the breast, they stick easily.

To assemble the dish, place the quail on lettuce on individual plates. Mix about 1 cup alfalfa with the grated carrot. Season with a little salt, pepper and some lemon juice. Form little mounds of the alfalfa, hollowing out the centre to make a nest and place these next to the quail. Put some quail eggs in each nest and decorate with a few violets.

Rabbit and Herb salad

Rabbit is perhaps rather neglected in the culinary world, yet when well prepared has more flavour than chicken and is equally tender. It needs to be roasted carefully for a salad so that it keeps moist.

This dish should not be refrigerated so cook the rabbit shortly before you intend to use it because chilling makes the meat firm and rather tasteless.

If you have the dressing ready and the bean and mushroom salad that accompanies it already prepared, it is quite simple to assemble the dish.

This is quite a substantial salad but if you want to serve something with it, choose either tiny potatoes cooked in their jackets and tossed with salt and pepper, or a plain potato salad.

Serve 4

1 × 1.5 kg (3 lb) rabbit
salt and pepper
several generous sprigs of
 thyme
250 g (8 oz) stringless green
 beans
1 tablespoon vegetable oil
125 g (4 oz) mushrooms
salt and pepper
butter lettuce
radicchio

Dressing:

2 hard-boiled eggs
2 teaspoons French or
 Dijon mustard
2 teaspoons dry,
 English-style mustard
1 cup (8 fl oz) vegetable oil
4 tablespoons red wine
 vinegar
2 tablespoons finely
 chopped parsley
2 tablespoons finely
 chopped chives
salt and pepper
2 teaspoons finely chopped
 fresh thyme

Season the rabbit well with salt and pepper and place the thyme into the cavity, pushing it down into the legs so it won't fall out during baking.

Place into a buttered ovenproof dish and cover with a thickly buttered piece of foil. Cook in a moderate oven, 180°C (350°F/Gas 4), until quite tender. It should take between 1 and $1\frac{1}{4}$ hours.

Remove and leave to cool slightly, tucking the foil over firmly to keep it moist.

Cut all the flesh from the bones and cut it into small pieces. Cut the liver into thin slices.

To make the dressing, mash the eggs, mix in the two mustards. Add the oil, vinegar, parsley, chives and salt and pepper. Mix well and then divide in half. Leave one half plain and add thyme to the other.

While the rabbit pieces are still slightly warm mix them with the dressing that has the thyme added. Marinate at least 1 hour to allow the dressing to soak in.

Cut the ends from the beans and cut into pieces about 5 cm (2 inches) long. Cook in boiling, salted water until just tender but still slightly crisp.

Remove, drain and refresh under cold water so they will retain their texture and colour.

If the mushrooms are large, cut in quarters, if small leave them whole.

Heat the oil in a frying pan. Add the mushrooms, season and cook over high heat for a couple of minutes until slightly softened.

Mix with the beans and the remainder of the dressing. Marinate for at least 1 hour.

Before placing on the platter, stir both the rabbit and the beans, coating them well so they will be quite moist.

To assemble, arrange a layer of butter lettuce around the edge of a large platter. Place a few pieces of radicchio between the lettuce leaves for added colour. Arrange a ring of the bean and mushroom salad inside the lettuce and fill the centre with the rabbit salad.

Place a couple of sprigs of fresh thyme on top to garnish, if you wish.

Pasta and Caviar salad with scallops (page 109)

Salad of Baby Onions and Pasta (page 109)

Curried Pilaf of Rice in Tomato Shells (page 108)

Rice and Shellfish salad

There is a vast difference in the flavour of rice that has been cooked in stock compared to rice cooked in water.

It is quite simple to make a stock from the liquid used to cook the scallops and prawns in this salad, and the rice will be lightly flavoured so it will need almost no dressing at all.

You need to use green prawns for this dish but if you can't obtain these, buy some cooked prawns, shell them and then simmer the shells in the wine and water for about 10 minutes to flavour it.

I have suggested using scallops and prawns, but other shellfish, such as crab, lobster, yabbies and Moreton Bay lobster, could be substituted.

Little else is needed with this dish other than a green salad. It would also make a lovely first course and the quantity would then extend to eight.

Serves 4

250 g (8 oz) scallops
375 g (12 oz) green prawns
  in the shell
1½ cups (12 fl oz) water
1½ cups (12 fl oz) dry white
  wine
small handful parsley,
  including a few stalks
3 tablespoons vegetable or
  olive oil

1 white onion, finely diced
1½ cups (12 oz) long grain
  rice
½ cup grated carrot

Dressing:
⅓ cup (2½ fl oz) olive oil
1 tablespoon lemon juice
1 ripe medium-sized
  tomato, peeled

Prepare the shellfish first so you can use the liquid to cook the rice.

Heat the water and wine with the parsley. Season with salt and pepper.

Clean the scallops and remove the little black section but retain the coral.

When the liquid has come to the boil, add the scallops and simmer for about 1 or 2 minutes, depending on their size. Be careful not to overcook them.

Remove with a slotted spoon and place on a plate. Place another plate on top to prevent them becoming dry.

Add the prawns to the same liquid and cook for about 3 minutes if the prawns are small, 5 if they are large.

Remove and leave to cool. When they have cooled, peel the prawns, remove the black vein and return the heads to the liquid. Cover and simmer gently for about 10 minutes.

Strain the liquid and measure out 3 cups. If it is not sufficient, add water to bring it up to the right amount.

In a saucepan, heat the oil and fry the onion for a few minutes, stirring continuously, until it has softened slightly.

Push the onion to one side of the pan and add the rice. Fry the rice, giving it an occasional stir, until the grains have changed from translucent to opaque.

Tip in the stock, check the seasoning, and as soon as it comes to the boil, cover and simmer gently. The rice will absorb all the liquid and become fluffy but the grains will remain separate. During the last 5 minutes of cooking, add the grated carrot.

When the rice is ready, place into a basin and fluff up lightly with 2 forks.

Cut the scallops in half if they are large.

Cut each prawn into pieces if they are large; if they are small, leave them whole. Add the shellfish to the rice.

Mix the oil and lemon juice. Cut the tomato into tiny pieces, discard some of the seeds and drain away any liquid that collects. Add to the oil and lemon and whisk well for a moment. Stir the dressing through the salad and mix lightly.

Cool, and serve at room temperature.

Curried Pilaf of Rice in Tomato Shells

A great many rice salads would not have much flavour if it were not for the dressing. This rice doesn't need any dressing at all, the method of cooking gives it sufficient flavour.

Mounded in tomato shells and with fine shreds of egg on the side, it is sufficient for a meal. However, if you wish you could serve it with either thin slices of ham, rare beef or prawns.

Serves 4

4 tomatoes
3 tablespoons vegetable oil
1 onion, finely diced
1 clove garlic, crushed
1 cup (8 oz) long grain rice
2 teaspoons Madras curry
  powder
2 cups (16 fl oz) chicken
  stock

1 cinnamon stick
1 tablespoon sultanas

Egg mixture:
1 tablespoon oil
2 eggs and 1 tablespoon
  water
salt and pepper
lettuce, to garnish

Place the tomatoes into a basin. Pour boiling water over them and leave for 10 seconds. Remove from the water and then peel away the skins. Cut the tomatoes in half.

Using a teaspoon or pressing down gently with your fingers, squeeze out the seeds and press down on the centre of each tomato so it forms an indented little case. Set aside. There is no need to chill them.

In a frying pan, heat the oil, add the onion and garlic and sauté for a few minutes or until slightly softened.

Add the rice and fry a moment in the oil, add the curry powder and then the stock. Bring the liquid to the boil and add the cinnamon stick and sultanas. Season the stock. Cover the pan and simmer gently until the rice has absorbed all the liquid but is cooked through. Remove from the heat and take out the cinnamon stick. Leave the rice to cool.

While the rice is cooking, prepare the egg mixture. Beat the eggs with the water and a little salt and pepper. Heat the oil in a frying pan, add the eggs and cook gently, as you would for an omelette, until the mixture is set.

Remove from the pan, roll up the omelette and then cut it into fine shreds.

Fill the tomatoes with the cooled rice, mounding it slightly. Spoon the left-over rice along the centre of a large oval platter. Place the lettuce leaves around the rice and scatter the egg strips over the lettuce. Arrange the filled tomatoes so that they sit easily in the rice.

This salad is best served at room temperature, so don't make it more than 4 or 5 hours in advance.

Pasta and Caviar salad with Scallops

Although scallops are suggested in the recipe, you could use any other shellfish, such as prawns, mussels, pieces of lobster or oysters.

The shellfish is moistened with mayonnaise, which is first lightened with a little of the cooking liquid from the scallops. The mayonnaise is also mixed with the pasta; so it shouldn't be too thick or it will make the salad slightly sticky and heavy.

To keep the dish as light as possible, leave the cooked tagliatelle or taglierini standing in water. This keeps the strands separate and is the most successful way of handling it—unless of course you cook the pasta at the last moment and quickly cool it.

Depending on appetites, you can cook a little more pasta than the amount given. The best accompaniment is a mixed green salad.

Serves 4

500 g (1 lb) scallops	2 teaspoons finely chopped
1 cup (8 fl oz) dry white	capers
wine	salt and pepper
1 cup (8 fl oz) water	$\frac{3}{4}$ cup (6 oz) oil mayonnaise
1 teaspoon salt	125 g (4 oz) white or green
generous sprig parsley	tagliatelle or taglierini
250 g (8 oz) ripe tomatoes,	45 g ($1\frac{1}{2}$ oz) pink caviar
peeled	finely chopped parsley

Trim the scallops and remove the little dark section from the side. Keep the coral.

Heat the wine, water, salt and parsley. Simmer 1 minute, add the scallops and cook gently for about 1 minute if small, 2 minutes if large. The mixture should not boil at any stage.

Drain, but keep the liquid. Place this back on the heat to reduce slightly. Set aside. Place the scallops on a plate; place another on top to keep them moist.

Cut the tomatoes into tiny pieces and discard the seeds and any juice which collects on the chopping board.

Add the capers to the tomatoes and mix in the scallops.

Add a little scallop cooking liquid to the mayonnaise and moisten the scallops with this. You don't need a great deal, about $\frac{1}{4}$ cup (2 fl oz) should be plenty.

Cover and store, refrigerated, for up to 8 hours.

Heat a large saucepan of water, adding a generous amount of salt and a spoonful of oil. When boiling, add the pasta, stir for a few seconds and leave to cook over high heat.

Taste. Don't have the pasta too 'al dente'—it is not quite so pleasant when cold.

When ready, drain. Run a little cold water over the top to stop it cooking. Place in a bowl of cold water and leave to stand. It can remain in this for several hours if necessary.

Shortly before using, drain well. Mix with the remainder of the mayonnaise and season with some pepper. Don't add salt as the caviar will be sufficiently salty.

Once the mayonnaise is added to the pasta, serve the salad within about 10 minutes or it will become too heavy.

Arrange the pasta in a circle, either on individual plates or a large platter. Place the scallop salad in the centre. Sprinkle the scallops with finely chopped parsley.

Carefully, and as evenly as possible, place caviar around the pasta.

Salad of Baby Onions and Pasta

In this salad, the onions are cooked in a wine mixture and the liquid is then mixed into pasta along with baby onions and sultanas.

Served with ham, it makes a substantial main dish and although the pasta should be cooked on the day it is to be eaten, the onions will keep well for 48 hours in the refrigerator.

Serves 4

24 tiny white onions	sprig of fresh thyme
1 cup (8 fl oz) dry white	1 tablespoon tomato paste
wine	$\frac{1}{2}$ cup (4 oz) sultanas
$\frac{1}{2}$ cup (4 fl oz) water	185 g (6 oz) small
1 tablespoon sugar	macaroni
1 clove garlic	2 large green peppers
1 bay leaf	(capsicums)
$\frac{1}{4}$ cup (2 fl oz) olive oil	salt and pepper
1 teaspoon salt	8 slices ham

Place the onions into a bowl and pour boiling water over them. Peel them and cut away the ends but leave a little of the root end on so that they remain whole.

Place the wine, water, sugar, garlic, bay leaf, oil, salt and thyme into a saucepan and bring to the boil.

Add the onions and simmer gently until they are tender. You may need to turn them over in the liquid as they cook. Don't cover the pan completely, tilt the lid slightly so that some steam can escape.

When the onions are just tender, add the tomato paste and mix through carefully. Add the sultanas and simmer another 5 minutes. Remove to a bowl to cool.

Cook the macaroni in a large pan of salted boiling water until it is tender. Drain well and rinse with cold water.

Cut the peppers in half, remove the seeds and press the peppers down to flatten them slightly so they will grill evenly.

Grill until the skin has darkened and blistered.

Remove, and when cool enough to handle, peel away the transparent skin, or as much of it as you can. Cut the peppers into small dice.

Place the pasta and peppers in a bowl.

Strain the onions but reserve the cooking liquid. If it is too thin, boil rapidly to reduce slightly and concentrate the flavour.

Remove the garlic, bay leaf and sprig of thyme and add the onions and sultanas to the macaroni.

Spoon over some of the cooking liquid from the onions to completely moisten the mixture. If too mild, add a teaspoon of either white vinegar or lemon juice. (Be sure to keep the remainder of the cooking liquid because you may need to add a little more to the pasta before serving. Usually, about $\frac{1}{2}$ to $\frac{3}{4}$ cup is sufficient but it can vary.)

Cover the pasta and let it stand at room temperature.

When ready to serve, cut the ham slices in halves or quarters; either roll over, or form into small cones and arrange around the outside of the salad. Add more liquid to the pasta if it has become dry, then spoon the pasta and onions into the centre of the platter.

Accompaniments

Egg Mayonnaise salad

One of the secrets of a good egg salad seems to be not to have the dressing or mayonnaise too thick. Instead of a light, fresh dish which can be part of an hors d'oeuvres or a mixed salad platter, it becomes too rich and heavy. While this makes an excellent first course it can also be served as an accompaniment to ham and poached sausage.

Serves 4

Garnish:

6 hard-boiled eggs
3 tablespoons vegetable oil
1 tablespoon white wine vinegar
2 tablespoons oil mayonnaise
1 tablespoon cream
salt and pepper

2 tablespoons capers, drained
$\frac{1}{2}$ bunch watercress or mustard and cress

Cut the eggs into thin slices.

Mix the oil, vinegar, mayonnaise, cream and seasoning. Spread a little of the mixture over the base of a platter. It should have a runny consistency.

Arrange the egg slices on top of this. Spoon more of the dressing on top; it won't cover the egg, some should show through the top.

Cut the capers in half, or smaller, and scatter on top.

Wash the watercress, or mustard and cress, and remove the pieces of watercress from the stalks. Place a layer around the egg salad.

Bean shoot and Egg strand salad

Fine shreds of omelette are often used as a garnish on Oriental dishes or fried rice.

It is used here in a salad with bean shoots and onion and although it may sound strange, it has a lovely lightness which makes it most suitable as an accompaniment to white meat.

Serves 4

Dressing:

250 g bean shoots
2 tablespoons vegetable oil
1 large white onion, sliced in thin half-slices
1 tablespoon sesame seeds
2 eggs
1 tablespoon water
$\frac{1}{4}$ teaspoon salt

2 teaspoons sesame oil
2 tablespoons vegetable oil
1 teaspoon sugar
1 tablespoon white vinegar
salt and pepper

Pinch off the tiny root end of the bean shoots. Place the bean shoots into a basin, pour boiling water over them and leave for about a minute. Drain and refresh immediately in cold water.

Heat the oil in a frying pan, add the onion and cook over a fairly high heat, stirring occasionally, until it has become slightly limp. Be careful not to let it brown.

Remove the onion and put the sesame seeds into the same pan. There will be sufficient oil left to fry them. Cook a minute until they are lightly coloured and then mix with the onions and bean shoots.

Beat the eggs with the water and salt.

Heat just enough oil to lightly coat the base of a frying pan.

Add sufficient egg to form a very thin layer, tilting the pan so the egg flows to the edges. Keep the heat very low and cook the egg until firm.

Depending on the size of the pan, you will be able to make 2 or 3 omelettes. The most important point to remember is to keep them thin.

When firm, ease a plastic eggslice or spatula underneath and remove to a plate to cool.

Roll each one over firmly and cut into fine shreds. Separate these and mix with the bean shoots and onions.

Mix the dressing ingredients together and whisk with a fork, or shake in a jar.

Pour the dressing over the salad and toss gently.

Watercress salad with Bacon and Egg

Watercress, either on its own or in combination with lettuce, makes a fine salad to accompany meats.

You will find that there is always some wastage; the heavy untidy stalk is not used in salads and any little yellowing sections should also be removed.

Pinch the sprigs to remove them from the stems, and store them in a plastic bag. The watercress will keep for a couple of days if sprinkled with a little water and kept chilled.

This salad is quite simple; the cress is sprinkled with some bacon and egg on top, but the flavours have a great affinity with the cress.

Cook the bacon as close to serving time as possible, although the dressing can be made and the egg chopped beforehand.

Serves 4

	Dressing:
1 bunch watercress	$\frac{1}{3}$ cup ($2\frac{1}{2}$ fl oz) vegetable or
90 g (3 oz) bacon, cut in	olive oil
tiny strips	1 tablespoon lemon juice
2 hard-boiled eggs	1 teaspoon sugar
	1 teaspoon Dijon mustard

Wash the watercress well and remove the sprigs from the stems.

Bunches vary in size but you need about 3 cups of loosely-packed watercress sprigs.

Place the bacon into a dry frying pan and cook, stirring until the fat is transparent and the bacon slightly crisp. Drain on kitchen paper.

Chop the egg into tiny pieces.

To make the dressing, add the lemon juice gradually to the oil, stirring constantly, then mix in the sugar and mustard.

Place the cress into a bowl and add the dressing. Toss lightly. Scatter the bacon and egg on top and serve immediately.

Tomato and Anchovy salad

A dish to make in the summer or autumn when you can get fresh basil, and sun-ripened tomatoes that have a full, sweet flavour.

The slightly pungent anchovy is good with the tomato slices alone, or accompanied by slices of hard-boiled eggs.

You can serve this salad as a first course or to accompany a plainly cooked or grilled meat dish.

Serves 4

4 medium-sized ripe	1 tablespoon fresh, finely
tomatoes	chopped basil
salt	black pepper
6 anchovies	a few fresh basil leaves to
3 tablespoons olive oil	garnish

Cut the tomatoes into thin slices and place on a plate or a board. Sprinkle with a little table salt and leave to stand for about 30 minutes. Don't oversalt because the anchovy will provide plenty.

Drain away the moisture that collects around the tomatoes.

Mash the anchovies. You should have about 1 table-spoonful. Mix with the oil, basil and a little black pepper.

Place a layer of tomato into a small, shallow bowl. Sprinkle a little of the anchovy mixture over the top. Continue adding the anchovy and tomato in layers, ending with a layer of anchovy.

Leave in a cool place (not the refrigerator as it will chill the dish too much) and let it stand for about another 30 minutes. You can leave it standing longer but the tomatoes will exude more liquid, which you will need to drain away.

Before serving, garnish with a few fresh basil leaves.

Tomatoes with Pesto

The Genoese invented pesto, the aromatic mixture that has a base of basil and adds flavour to pasta, soups, or vegetables. It is quite simple but, like so many simple things, it needs the best products to develop its special fragrance.

Fresh basil, freshly grated cheese, not the pre-grated variety, good quality olive oil and, as the Genoese say, a strong arm and a marble mortar.

It is possibly true that grinding the basil in a pestle and mortar releases more flavour, but nowadays it is usually made in a food processor. It may not be quite as good, but is still aromatic—and takes a quarter of the time.

In Genoa the Parmesan cheese is usually mixed with a tangy Sardinian cheese but since this variety of cheese is not always easy to obtain, I make this using only Parmesan.

The mixture is spread over the top of the tomatoes to coat the surface completely, then garnished with a fresh basil leaf on top.

Pesto is so well-flavoured that it goes best with plain meat dishes, but it could be served as an hors d'oeuvre instead.

Serves 6

750 g ($1\frac{1}{2}$ lb) ripe tomatoes	2 tablespoons pine nuts
salt and pepper	$\frac{1}{3}$ cup ($1\frac{1}{2}$ oz) finely grated
1 cup lightly packed fresh	Parmesan cheese
basil leaves	$\frac{1}{2}$ cup (4 fl oz) olive oil
1 small clove garlic,	lettuce
crushed	some additional small fresh
	basil leaves to garnish

Cut the tomatoes into slices, discarding the end pieces. The slices should be about 1 cm ($\frac{1}{2}$ inch) thick.

Season lightly with salt and pepper and leave them to stand for about 30 minutes, draining away any moisture that accumulates.

Place the basil, garlic, pine nuts, cheese and oil into a blender or food processor and process until it forms a green purée. It should be thick enough to coat the back of a spoon.

Place a spoonful on top of each tomato slice, spreading it to the edges.

As it stands it will change colour and become darker but this will not affect the flavour. However, once it is assembled, it is best eaten within a couple of hours.

Arrange some flat lettuce leaves on a platter, place the tomato slices on top, and decorate each one with a basil leaf.

Cabbage salad with Sesame seeds (page 128)

Vegetable salad with Peanut sauce (page 117)

Spiced salad (page 121)

Watercress salad with Bacon and Egg (page 113)

Salad with Baby Squash and Tomatoes

In some countries these little baby green squash are known as custard marrow. They are a particularly attractive vegetable, their edges curved into scallops and the palest green in colour.

They are best when small and are perfect about the size of a small apricot.

In a salad they are not successful raw or steamed because they lack flavour, but lightly fried they have an interesting texture and taste.

They combine well with tomatoes and herbs but when tomatoes are not in season, slices of young zucchini could be fried and layered through the salad instead.

Serves 4

	Dressing:
500 g (1 lb) tiny green squash	$\frac{1}{3}$ cup ($2\frac{1}{2}$ fl oz) olive oil
2 tablespoons vegetable oil (or more if needed)	1 tablespoon lemon juice
1 clove garlic, crushed	2 tablespoons finely chopped basil
375 g (12 oz) ripe tomatoes, peeled	1 teaspoon finely chopped fresh thyme
1 small white onion, finely diced	
salt and pepper	

Cut the squash into fairly thin slices.

Heat a little oil in a frying pan and add a layer of the squash. Cook over a medium heat, turning once. They should be tender and tinged with gold on the outside, but still crisp.

As each layer is cooked, drain on kitchen paper and add another layer, until all the squash are cooked.

Cut the tomato into thin slices, at the same time shaking out some of the seeds.

In a shallow serving dish or platter, place first a layer of tomato, then a layer of squash, a scattering of onion, salt and pepper, and so on.

Mix together all the dressing ingredients and whisk with a fork.

Pour the dressing over the salad and leave to stand for about 30 minutes. It can be left longer if necessary but the excess liquid which accumulates will have to be drained away before serving.

Vegetable salad with Basil and fresh Tomato sauce

Although this vegetable salad could include any vegetables that are in season, it relies on two ingredients to make it a summer-autumn dish—ripe, well-flavoured tomatoes and fresh basil. During winter tomatoes are often floury and would not have sufficient flavour, and only the fresh basil gives the right seasoning.

The vegetables listed in the recipe are only meant to be a guide-line. Use any freshly picked vegetables that are in season and at their peak, remembering that a variation in colour will add interest to the dish.

As in all types of cooking, the look is important. Smaller points such as cutting the carrot into fine julienne strips instead of slices, the

beans into neat pieces, and using only the baby flowerets of cauliflower or broccoli, all make a great difference to the result.

Serves 4

	Dressing:
125 g (4 oz) stringless beans	1 large ripe tomato, weighing about 185 g (6 oz)
125 g (4 oz) young carrots	
100 g ($3\frac{1}{2}$ oz) snow peas	1 tablespoon finely chopped shallots (or spring onions)
1 cup cauliflower or broccoli flowerets	
6 spring onions (scallions)	1 tablespoon finely chopped basil
	1 tablespoon finely chopped parsley
	1 teaspoon French mustard
	$\frac{1}{3}$ cup ($2\frac{1}{2}$ fl oz) olive oil
	1 tablespoon red wine vinegar
	$\frac{1}{2}$ teaspoon sugar
	salt and pepper

Cook the vegetables first. The beans, carrots, peas and spring onions can be cooked together, but remember to place them in the water at different times because some will take less cooking time than others.

Remove the ends from the beans and then cut into small, neat pieces.

Scrape the carrots and cut them into julienne strips about the size of large matchsticks.

Remove both ends from the snow peas and pull away the string.

Cut the spring onions into chunky pieces.

Cook the beans and carrots in a pan of boiling salted water for about 5 to 6 minutes.

The snow peas and spring onions will take only 1 or 2 minutes to cook.

Cook the cauliflower or broccoli separately because of their strong flavour. They will also need about 5 minutes.

When the vegetables are cooked, but still slightly crunchy, drain them well and run cold water over them to refresh them and retain their bright colours. Drain well.

Pour the dressing over the salad and leave to stand for at least 1 hour, although the salad can be kept for 5 to 6 hours if necessary.

To make the dressing, peel the tomato by plunging it into boiling water for about 10 seconds. Cut it into tiny pieces. Don't discard all the seeds and juice, but shake some away or the dressing will be too thin.

Crush the tomato pieces slightly and place into a basin with the shallots, basil, parsley, mustard, olive oil, vinegar and sugar and season with salt and pepper.

Mix well before pouring it over the salad and then stir the salad before serving.

Vegetable salad with Peanut sauce

This dish is interesting enough to serve as a first course, especially if you add a couple of prawns as a garnish on each portion.

It is very well-flavoured so if used as an accompaniment it needs to be served with a plain steak or chicken dish rather than anything which has a sauce.

Serves 4

	Peanut Sauce:
125 g (4 oz) snow peas	**1 clove garlic, crushed**
125 g (4 oz) bean shoots	**2 tablespoons light soy**
1 small white onion, cut in	** sauce**
** thin half slices (see note)**	**3 tablespoons peanut butter**
1 cup finely shredded	**1 small dried chilli**
** Chinese cabbage**	**2 teaspoons sugar**
Note: If you don't like serving	**1 cup water**

raw onions, or would prefer a milder flavour, you can toss the onion in a little oil for a few minutes before adding to the salad. The flavour will be different but still good.

Remove the ends from the snow peas and pull away any string from the back.

Place into a saucepan of boiling salted water and bring to the boil again. Cook only a few seconds, remove, drain and refresh under cold running water. Drain on some kitchen paper.

Pinch the tiny root end from the bean shoots.

Mix together the snow peas, bean shoots, onion and cabbage.

Arrange on a shallow platter rather than in a bowl. Cover and keep refrigerated until you are ready to serve the salad.

Place all the ingredients for the peanut sauce into a small saucepan and bring to the boil. Cook gently for about 5 minutes or until the sauce has thickened slightly. Leave to cool. If you find when it has cooled that it has become too thick, heat again with a few more spoonfuls of water. Remove the chilli before using the sauce.

Serve the peanut sauce at the table.

Lettuce with Avocado Dressing

This pale green dressing is rich, but it is lightened slightly by lemon juice. Some additional avocado slices are served with the lettuce salad and small cherry tomatoes are scattered on top to give some fresh flavour and colour. If you can't obtain cherry tomatoes, a few peeled wedges of tomato can be substituted.

Although avocado has a habit of darkening, this dressing can be kept covered for about 6 hours without coming to any harm. The avocado half to be used for the salad should be kept tightly wrapped. If you leave the stone in the centre, it helps to prevent discolouration.

I find the dressing occasionally becomes too thick. It may sound strange, but it is best thinned with a spoonful of milk or you could use more lemon juice. Be cautious however, that you don't make it too sharp.

Serves 4

	Dressing:
1 mignonette lettuce	**$\frac{1}{2}$ avocado weighing**
18 sprigs from the pale	** approximately 100 g ($3\frac{1}{2}$**
** yellow part of endive**	** oz)**
$\frac{1}{2}$ avocado	**1 tablespoon lemon juice**
8 cherry tomatoes	**1 tablespoon mayonnaise**
	$\frac{1}{3}$ cup ($2\frac{1}{2}$ fl oz) cream
	salt and pepper

First make the dressing. Peel the avocado and place into a food processor or blender with the lemon juice. Blend until smooth. Add the mayonnaise, cream, salt and pepper. If it is too thick, thin with a little milk.

Wash the mignonette and dry well. Place into a bowl with the endive pieces. Spoon the avocado dressing over the top. Peel the avocado and cut into long thin strips. Arrange these on top of the salad. Cut the cherry tomatoes in half and scatter on top.

Sweet Carrot salad

This salad is colourful, healthy and a lot tastier than most carrot salads.

The sweetness comes not only from the carrots but also from the sultanas that are mixed through it.

Serves 4

	Dressing:
$\frac{1}{3}$ cup sultanas (raisins)	**$\frac{1}{3}$ cup ($2\frac{1}{2}$ fl oz) vegetable**
400 g (13 oz) young carrots	** oil**
$\frac{1}{4}$ cup roughly chopped	**1 tablespoon lemon juice**
** walnuts**	**salt and pepper**
3 tablespoons finely	
** chopped parsley**	

Place the sultanas into a bowl and pour boiling water over them. Leave to stand for about 5 minutes, then drain.

Grate the carrots on a medium to fine grater.

Place the carrots into a bowl with the sultanas, walnuts and parsley and mix with the dressing.

To make the dressing, mix the ingredients in a bowl, whisking until thick, or shake them in a jar.

Leave the salad to stand for about 30 minutes before serving. However, you could leave it for 3 to 4 hours if necessary and it will still taste fine.

White Bean salad with Herbs and Vegetables

Small white beans, which the French call haricot and the Americans navy beans, are used extensively for stews because they keep a good shape and flavour, without becoming too soft.

A high source of protein, they are very satisfying, either eaten as a small course on their own, or with a meat dish.

You could store beans indefinitely but as time passes they become increasingly drier and lose flavour so it is best not to keep them for more than a few months. Of course, it is often impossible to know how long they may have been stored in the shops.

Combined with vegetables, they make a lovely salad and this is one dish in which a good olive oil should be used because its flavour seems to have a great affinity with the beans.

Serves 4–6

1 cup (8 oz) white haricot beans
1 large sprig thyme
$\frac{1}{4}$ cup finely chopped spring onion (scallions)
$\frac{1}{2}$ cup sliced or diced carrot
250 g (8 oz) ripe tomatoes, peeled
2 tablespoons finely chopped parsley
2 tablespoons finely chopped fresh basil
1 teaspoon finely chopped fresh thyme

Dressing:
$\frac{1}{2}$ cup (4 fl oz) olive oil
2 tablespoons white wine vinegar
salt and pepper

Cover the beans in water and soak overnight. If, however, they are new season's beans, a few hours will be sufficient.

Drain and add fresh water. Don't salt the water now as this toughens the beans.

Add the sprig of thyme and simmer the beans gently until almost tender. Add salt and continue cooking until tender.

Drain the beans and add the spring onion.

Cook the carrot in salted water until just tender. Drain and mix into the beans.

Dice the tomato into small pieces, discarding some of the seeds, and mix through the parsley, basil and thyme.

To make the dressing, whisk the oil and vinegar with a fork, or shake in a jar. Season well. If you like, you can add a crushed clove of garlic to make the salad more pungent. However, the herbs add considerable flavour so it is a matter of personal taste.

Stir the dressing into the salad and let it stand for 20 minutes before serving.

You can make the salad several hours beforehand but the herbs should be added shortly before serving so that they will retain their fresh green colour.

Lettuce with Avocado dressing (page 117)

Watercress salad (page 121)

Parsley and Herb salad (page 120)

Salad of Three Beans

There is such a variety of bean salads sold in tins or available from take-away food shops that I hesitated even to include a recipe. However, there is a vast difference between the ready-prepared salads and the fresh-tasting home-made ones.

The green beans need to be cooked for this recipe but the tinned kidney and canneloni beans are fine to use. The most important point to remember is not only to drain the beans but to rinse away the liquid around them, before coating with fresh dressing.

Serves 6 to 8
250 g stringless green beans
1 × 310 g (10 oz) tin kidney beans
1 × 310 g (10 oz) tin canneloni beans
1 white onion, finely chopped
1 clove garlic, crushed

Dressing:
½ cup (4 fl oz) vegetable oil
2 tablespoons red wine vinegar
generous pinch dried thyme, or 2 teaspoons fresh thyme
2 tablespoons finely chopped parsley
few drops Tabasco
1 tablespoon sweet-sour cucumber, finely chopped
1 teaspoon sugar

Top and tail the beans and cut them into small, neat pieces.

Place into boiling salted water and cook over rapid heat until barely tender. They should only take about 6 minutes but taste one to check them.

Remove and refresh under cold running water to prevent further cooking and to retain the colour.

Drain the kidney and canneloni beans and rinse them. Leave to drain.

Mix all the beans with the onion and garlic.

Mix together all the dressing ingredients by either whisking them or shaking them in a jar.

Coat the beans thoroughly with the dressing.

Stand the salad for 1 hour before serving, although it can be kept for several hours. Refrigerate in warm weather.

After about 12 hours the green beans will lose some of their colour but the salad will still taste good.

Parsley and Herb salad

Used as a garnish for so many different dishes because of its bright and fresh green colour, parsley is also a valuable source of vitamins.

Although not so common as a salad green, it makes an interesting accompaniment or it could be served after a rich main course.

I like to use two types of parsley, the flat-leaf Continental parsley, sometimes known as Italian parsley, along with some of the more familiar curly parsley.

Combined with garden herbs, it is also good with a cheese course.

When measuring the parsley, remove the leaves and pack them down quite firmly into the cup.

Salad Burnet has a delicate lacy foliage and its fragile appearance belies its hardy nature. It can be easily grown at home either in a small pot or in a vegetable garden and the leaves have a light nutty flavour.

There is no substitute for this so if not obtainable make the salad without it.

Serves 4
1 cup Continental (flat-leaf) parsley sprigs
½ cup curly parsley sprigs
20 small basil leaves
4 stalks salad burnet
4 inside pale yellow celery tops
8 small lettuce leaves

Dressing:
1 small clove garlic, crushed
3 tablespoons olive oil
3 teaspoons lemon juice
1 teaspoon red wine vinegar
salt and pepper

Place both types of parsley into a bowl. Add the basil leaves.

Remove the leaves from the salad burnet and mix them with the parsley.

Break off the pale yellow celery tops and mix them in.

Tear the lettuce into small pieces and add to the salad.

This can be covered and kept in a crisper to chill but mix in the dressing only at the last moment and serve immediately.

To make the dressing, mix the garlic with the oil. Gradually add the lemon and vinegar, whisking with a fork, or shake the mixture in a jar until thick. Season with salt and pepper.

Spiced salad

This salad could be served either in lettuce cups or in a small bowl.

It is crisp and crunchy and, with all the protein it contains in the few ingredients, could be classified as a 'health food'.

To retain the fresh, crisp taste, mix in the dressing just before serving. You could, however, make up the salad, cover and store it in the refrigerator some hours beforehand.

Serves 4

2 cups finely shredded
  Chinese cabbage
1 cup bean shoots
$\frac{1}{2}$ cup alfalfa sprouts
$\frac{1}{2}$ cup grated carrot

Dressing:

1 clove garlic, crushed
$\frac{1}{4}$ teaspoon salt
2 teaspoons sesame oil
1 tablespoon soy sauce
$\frac{1}{3}$ cup (2$\frac{1}{2}$ fl oz) vegetable
  oil
1 tablespoon white wine
  vinegar, or lemon juice
1 teaspoon finely chopped
  fresh chilli (see note)

Note: You can delete the chilli if you prefer a milder flavour. If you are using it, use only the outside, wash away the hot seeds and be certain to wash your hands well afterwards.

Since it is only a small amount of chilli, I find it rarely too hot for any guests; however personal tastes vary, as do the heat of individual chillies. If you are uncertain, it is safer to use less the first time and increase the amount later if you like.

Place the cabbage into a bowl. (You can include some of the white stalk end along with the green.)

Nip the tails from the bean shoots. Add the bean shoots, sprouts and carrot to the cabbage.

Mix all the dressing ingredients in a bowl and whisk with a fork.

Mix the dressing into the salad, and serve.

Watercress salad

The perfect place for this salad is after the main course. It is interesting served instead of cheese, since the shreds of cheese are spread through the cress and leave quite a definite flavour on your palate.

Grate the cheese shortly before serving and, if you wish, you could add more than the recipe states.

If you are drinking wine, you may prefer to use lemon juice instead of vinegar, so as not to spoil the taste of the wine, and then add a little extra oil to the dressing to keep the proportions correct.

Serves 4

$\frac{1}{2}$ bunch watercress
3 tablespoons finely grated
  tasty or a Cheddar-type
  cheese
12 small cherry tomatoes

Dressing:

3 tablespoons vegetable oil
1 tablespoon white wine
  vinegar
or
1 tablespoon lemon juice
salt and pepper

Remove the cress from the stalks, discarding any leaves that are discoloured or slightly damaged. It is a little hard to calculate how much you will have, since bunches vary, but you need at least 1 to 1$\frac{1}{2}$ cups firmly packed pieces for 4 people.

Place in the refrigerator to crisp.

Put the watercress into a bowl and add the cheese, lifting the cress either with forks or your fingers, to mix thoroughly. Add the dressing and toss lightly.

To make the dressing, whisk the oil and vinegar (or lemon juice) with a fork, or shake in a jar. Season. Be a little cautious with the salt as the cheese adds some to the dish.

Cut the cherry tomatoes in half and arrange around the edge of a dish. Place the watercress in the centre.

Once the salad is mixed it must be served at once.

Tabbouleh

This most famous of Lebanese salads, tasting of fresh lemon and parsley, is rich in vitamins and minerals.

However, it falls into the category of 'a little seems to go a long way' and in Lebanon is served as a first course or part of a buffet.

It has a refreshing quality and is very good with barbecued or plain meats. It is most important to get the lemon taste just right— not overpowering, yet definitely noticeable on the palate. Lemons vary in acidity, depending on the variety, so let your taste buds determine how much you should use.

The cracked wheat is obtainable from most health food stores.

The directions on the cracked wheat packets usually suggest soaking it for about 30 minutes, until the grain has split and is puffed. I have found this length of time to be insufficient with some of the brands I have tried so you may have to soak the wheat for much longer.

If you find you are using a wheat that becomes soft after a shorter soaking time, drain immediately, squeeze out the moisture and store in the refrigerator, covered. It will not spoil if it has to wait a short time until you are ready to make the salad.

Serves 4

155 g (5 oz) cracked wheat
  (burghul)
$\frac{1}{2}$ cup finely chopped
  spring onions (scallions)
375 g (12 oz) ripe tomatoes,
  peeled
1 cup finely chopped
  parsley
2 tablespoons finely
  chopped mint

Dressing:

2 tablespoons light olive oil
3 tablespoons lemon juice
salt and pepper

Soak the cracked wheat for about 6 to 8 hours, or overnight if necessary. Strain and squeeze out any excess water. Mix with the spring onions.

Chop the tomato into small pieces, discarding some of the seeds and juice.

Add the tomatoes to the cracked wheat and spring onions and mix in the parsley and mint.

Mix together the dressing ingredients. Mix the dressing into the salad and adjust the seasoning.

Cover and leave 1 hour to mature, or you can store it in the refrigerator for a day.

White Bean salad with Herbs and Vegetables (page 118)

Potato and Pea salad (page 132)

Broccoli and Macaroni salad (page 138)

Salad of Three Beans (page 120)

Cauliflower salad

When using cauliflower in a salad, it is very important that it is at the peak of the season. It should be barely creamy in colour with firm, close whorls that have a sweet, rather than a strong smell.

This dressing will soak into the cooked cauliflower which will become soft and tinged with pink.

Note that the paprika used is sweet, not hot, and is meant to give colour and a little flavour but no spice.

Grated radish is sprinkled over the top of the cauliflower before serving but you can omit this if you prefer the cauliflower plain. It does, however, give a pleasant, fresh taste which counteracts the slight sweetness of the sauce.

Serves 6
500 g (1 lb) cauliflower
3 or 4 radishes (optional)

Dressing:
3 tablespoons vegetable oil
1 tablespoon white wine vinegar
¼ cup (2 fl oz) mayonnaise
2 teaspoons sweet paprika
2 teaspoons tomato sauce (ketchup)
salt and pepper

Cut the little flowerets from the cauliflower. The stalk can be used but should be cut into thin slices. If there are any very large or tough sections, discard them.

Cook the cauliflower in a pan of salted water until just barely tender. The cooking time will largely depend on the freshness of the cauliflower, rather than its size, but about 5 minutes should be ample. Keep testing with a knife while it is cooking.

Drain and immediately refresh with cold water to prevent it cooking any further. Leave to drain and cool.

To make the dressing, add the vinegar to the oil, whisking with a fork. Mix in the mayonnaise, paprika, tomato sauce and seasoning.

Add the dressing to the cauliflower, stirring gently to coat it evenly. It will change to a pink colour. Cover, and if the weather is warm, refrigerate it.

Trim the ends from the radishes, put them into iced water and leave in the refrigerator.

When ready to serve the cauliflower, grate the radishes and scatter over the top.

Mushroom and Pepper salad

The small, firm button mushrooms are best for this salad. The darker, more open mushrooms become too soft and will often form liquid in the salad if it is left to stand.

It is important that the mushrooms are cut very thinly for the best flavour and appearance.

The amount may seem generous when you first slice the mushrooms but they reduce considerably in volume as the salad stands.

This salad is best with meat dishes or roast chicken.

Serves 4
250 g (8 oz) small, firm mushrooms
1 medium-sized red or green pepper (capsicum)
salt and pepper

Dressing:
⅓ cup (2½ fl oz) vegetable or olive oil
1 tablespoon white wine vinegar
1 small clove garlic, crushed

Cut the stems level with the mushroom caps or remove them if they are woody and tough.

Slice the mushrooms very thinly.

Cut the pepper in half and remove all the seeds. If the skin of the pepper is a bit thick, remove some of the inside sections.

Cut the pepper into very thin slices and then across so you have matchstick-sized pieces.

Mix with the mushrooms, seasoning with salt and pepper and add the dressing.

To make the dressing, mix the oil, vinegar and garlic and either whisk the mixture or shake in a jar until thick.

Stir well and let the salad stand for at least 1 hour, by which time the mushrooms will be soft. If you want to keep the salad longer, cover and refrigerate.

Cucumber salad with Yogurt and Mint

A typical salad from the Middle East, this is very refreshing in summer served with chicken or spiced meats.

It only makes a tiny bowl of salad but of course you can double the quantities if you feel you need more of the one type of salad.

Serves 4
1 large cucumber, weighing about 375 g (12 oz)
1 teaspoon salt
1 teaspoon sugar
1 tablespoon finely chopped spring onions (scallions)
1 tablespoon finely chopped fresh mint
¾ cup (6 fl oz) yogurt
black pepper

Peel the cucumber and cut it in half lengthwise. Using a teaspoon, remove the seeds.

Cut the cucumber into wafer-thin slices and place them in a bowl with the salt and sugar. Let it stand for at least 30 minutes. Drain well and squeeze any excess moisture from the cucumber.

Mix together the spring onions, mint, yogurt and black pepper.

Mix through the cucumber and chill in the refrigerator if not using immediately.

Don't leave this salad to stand for too long once the yogurt is mixed through. The cucumber will continue to expel moisture as it stands, making the salad limp and watery.

Zucchini salad

A lovely, light dish which could be served either as an accompaniment, or for a casual meal, as a first course.

The zucchini are first cooked by boiling gently, then coated with a sauce. As it is a rather watery vegetable, I had some reservations at first because I thought it might be too bland but it proved to be a very tasty dish, provided the zucchini are fresh and not too large.

Serves 4
4 medium-sized zucchini

Dressing:
1 small tomato, peeled

1 clove garlic, crushed
4 tablespoons olive oil
1 tablespoon red wine
  vinegar
salt and pepper

Place the washed zucchini in a saucepan of salted water. Bring to the boil and cook gently for about 10 minutes or until the zucchini are just tender when pierced with the point of a knife.

Drain and run cold water over them to prevent further cooking. Leave to cool.

Cut off both ends of the zucchinis then cut each into half and leave on kitchen paper to drain. This can be done beforehand but the dressing should be added only about 1 hour before serving otherwise the moisture that exudes from the zucchini will make the salad watery.

To make the dressing, cut the tomato into tiny pieces. Discard the seeds and drain off some of the juice. Crush the tomato with a fork. Add the garlic, mix in the oil, vinegar, salt and pepper and either whisk or stir until thick. If too sharp add a pinch of sugar.

Arrange the zucchini on a plate and spoon some dressing on top of each half.

Green salad with Hazelnuts

This salad is a mixture of greens—some mignonette lettuce (or you could use butter lettuce instead), spinach and parsley.

However, this is just a guideline as any mixture could be used, keeping the different greens in equal proportions.

Hazelnut oil is exquisite and worth buying even though it is quite expensive. A little goes a long way in a salad and you don't need to use all hazelnut; you could mix it with some light vegetable oil and still retain the flavour.

The vinegar taste is kept light because the nut taste should dominate; if you find the salad too oily for your palate, add another couple of teaspoons of vinegar or lemon juice to the dressing.

Serves 4
8 leaves mignonette lettuce
8 baby English spinach
  leaves
$\frac{1}{3}$ cup Continental or
  Italian parsley (leaves
  only)
45 g ($1\frac{1}{2}$ oz) hazelnuts

Dressing:
2 tablespoons hazelnut oil
2 tablespoons vegetable oil
1 tablespoon white wine
  vinegar
salt and pepper

Remove the back stalk and some of the back vein from the spinach but be careful to leave the leaf unbroken.

Remove all the stalks from the parsley and measure $\frac{1}{3}$ cup of leaves, firmly packed. Chill all the greens.

Place the hazelnuts on an oven tray and heat in a moderate oven for about 10 minutes until they are light golden and the skins crack and loosen. Rub the nuts in a tea towel to remove most of the skin. Cut into fine slices.

To make the dressing, mix the two oils and gradually whisk in the vinegar, or shake the mixture in a jar. Season with salt and pepper.

Mix the greens with dressing and scatter the nuts over the top. Serve immediately.

Mixed Green salad with Macadamia Nuts

Some years ago I read in a reference book on food that the macadamia was a 'native of Australia but a speciality of Hawaii'.

This is not so true now, for with the development of the macadamia nut industry in this country, our own product can be bought everywhere.

It has a rich, almost oily texture and although expensive, a small amount will give a lot of flavour.

It is lovely in a fresh green salad, served as an accompaniment to meat. This salad could be served as a course on its own, either before or after a main dish.

Serves 4
20 baby spinach leaves
90 g (3 oz) small firm
  mushrooms
salt and pepper
2 teaspoons lemon juice
$\frac{1}{2}$ cup alfalfa
8 lettuce leaves
60 g (2 oz) macadamia nuts

Dressing:
4 tablespoons vegetable or
  olive oil
2 teaspoons Worcestershire
  sauce
1 tablespoon white wine
  vinegar
salt and pepper

Wash the spinach and remove the stalks from each leaf. Chill the leaves.

Remove the stalks from the mushrooms. Cut the caps into thin slices and season with salt, pepper and a little lemon juice. Leave for about 15 minutes before using, although they can be left for longer if necessary.

Break the lettuce into small pieces and place in the refrigerator until crisp.

Cut the nuts into thin slices. Place either into the oven and cook until golden or toast them in a frying pan until lightly coloured.

Whisk together the oil, Worcestershire sauce and vinegar, or shake them in a jar. Add seasoning.

Place the spinach, mushrooms, alfalfa and lettuce into a bowl and toss with the dressing.

Scatter the nuts over the top.

Marinated Mixed Vegetables

Most dishes in which the vegetables are marinated have a strong taste of vinegar but this particular one is quite mild.

Any type of vegetable can be used, but look for different colours and textures.

There may seem to be quite a lot of liquid but they need to be well covered when stored so that they are not only well-flavoured but keep well.

Although they will still have a good texture, green vegetables lose some colour after a day in this marinade. They will keep for 3 days.

This dish is interesting with plain meats and is particularly good with grilled or roasted chicken.

Serves 4–6

125 g (4 oz) carrots	Marinade:
125 g (4 oz) green stringless beans	**3 cups (24 fl oz) water**
125 g (4 oz) cauliflower flowerets	**2 tablespoons sugar**
	3 whole garlic cloves
1 medium-sized cucumber	**1 tablespoon grated fresh ginger**
1 large white onion	**$\frac{1}{4}$ cup (2 fl oz) vegetable oil**
	$\frac{1}{3}$ cup (2$\frac{1}{2}$ fl oz) white wine vinegar
	salt and pepper

Peel the carrots and cut into julienne strips.

Remove the ends from the beans and cut into chunky pieces.

Cook the carrots, beans and cauliflower separately. They should take only a couple of minutes each. Drain well and refresh in cold water.

Peel the cucumber. Cut lengthwise and remove the seeds. Cut the cucumber into long strips. Place into cold water which is well salted. Bring to the boil and cook 1 minute. Drain. Cut the onion into slices or half-slices and cook as for the cucumber. Drain well.

Place all the vegetables into a bowl and pour the hot marinade over them.

To make the marinade, place all the ingredients into a saucepan. Bring to the boil, simmer, uncovered, for about 10 minutes. Strain.

Stand the vegetables for at least 6 hours before using although they can be kept for several days.

Marinated Onion salad

The longer you leave this salad the better it tastes. The onions will gradually soften in the marinade, developing colour and a lovely pickled flavour.

Make it in the morning if you wish to serve it in the evening and if you leave it a day or so, covered and refrigerated, it will improve still further.

It is best served as a side dish with barbecued meats or steak.

Serves 4

2 large white or Spanish onions	**2 tablespoons lemon juice**
	2 teaspoons sugar
	1 teaspoon cumin
Dressing:	**$\frac{1}{4}$ teaspoon turmeric**
$\frac{1}{3}$ cup (2$\frac{1}{2}$ fl oz) vegetable or olive oil	**salt and pepper**

Mix all the dressing ingredients, stirring them in a bowl or shaking them in a jar.

Cut the onions in half and place them flat side down. Cut them as thinly as you can, separating the rings a little, and place into a basin.

Add the dressing and stir to mix well. Leave 1 hour, stir again, then leave several hours. If the mixture is too wet, drain a little liquid away before serving.

Cucumber shreds with Green sauce

This is quite different to the usual cucumber salad because instead of slicing or dicing it, long thin shreds are removed from the cucumber, using a vegetable peeler. The salad almost has the appearance of fine strands of noodles.

This is a lovely side dish to serve with fish or shellfish.

Makes 4 small servings

2 large or 3 small cucumbers	Green Sauce:
salt	**1 cup watercress leaves**
1 teaspoon sugar	**2 tablespoons vegetable oil**
	3 teaspoons white wine vinegar
	1 teaspoon finely chopped dill
	salt and pepper

Peel the cucumber. Using a vegetable peeler, shred the flesh only (do not cut into the seedy centre) into fine, long shreds. They should be wafer thin. Place them on a plate, sprinkle with a little kitchen salt and the sugar and leave to stand for about 30 minutes.

Drain away the liquid. Rinse the cucumber and then drain well and pat dry with kitchen paper.

To make the dressing, place the watercress leaves and the oil into a blender. Don't chop the leaves first or they will fly around the container instead of being ground finely. Scrape down the sides and blend until it forms a pale green purée. Mix in the vinegar and dill and season with salt and pepper to taste.

Mix the cucumber in a bowl with the dressing, separating the strands lightly so that they are not packed down. Serve within 30 minutes.

You can have the dressing made and the cucumber ready beforehand but if made too early the cucumber will continue to accumulate liquid and the dish will become rather soggy.

Cauliflower salad (page 124)

Cucumber salad with Yogurt and Mint (page 124)

Green salad with Hazelnuts (page 124)

Spinach and Bacon salad

Some years ago children were served spoonfuls of cooked spinach, along with an admonition that every scrap must be eaten, in the belief that it supplied the iron and vitamins necessary for healthy growth.

It seems somewhat surprising that, until recently, it was rarely served as a salad, which makes it far more interesting and attractive.

Small leaves are best to use and they should be bright and fresh in appearance. Jane Grigson, a well-known English writer, describes it perfectly in her book on vegetables when she says that really fresh spinach makes the sounds 'crunch and squeak'.

Baby leaves can have the stalk removed at the base of the leaf but larger ones need to be pulled gently so they come away from the back. The way to do it is to hold the leaf doubled over firmly in your left hand and pull the stalk gently upwards with your right hand.

Discard any damaged or broken leaves to use in cooking.

The bacon is added warm and some of the fat, too, at the last moment. However, bacon varies considerably in fat content; if you have a pan full, use your discretion as to how much to use in the salad. This salad should really be served as a course completely on its own.

Serves 6–8

Dressing:

½ **bunch baby English spinach**
185 g (6 oz) small mushrooms
2 teaspoons lemon juice
125 g (4 oz) bacon, cut into fine strips
salt and pepper

3 tablespoons vegetable oil
½ **teaspoon sugar**
1 tablespoon white wine vinegar, or lemon juice

Wash the spinach well, using several changes of water. Drain well and chill.

Cut the mushrooms into thin slices, removing the stalks, unless they are very tiny. Place in a small bowl and add the lemon juice. Stir to coat and let it stand for about 20 minutes to soften slightly.

Place the bacon into a pan and sauté, stirring occasionally, until it is crisp and the fat transparent. You must do this at the last moment; the bacon should be warm when added to the salad. You can, however, partly cook it beforehand and then reheat it just before serving.

Whisk all the dressing ingredients, or shake in a jar.

Place the spinach into a bowl and toss with some dressing. Season (be a little cautious with salt).

Scatter the mushrooms over the top.

Add the bacon, distributing it as evenly as possible, spooning over a little of the bacon fat.

Mixed shredded salad

Although all the ingredients in this salad are not actually shredded —the carrots and white radish are grated—they look as if they have all been cut in a similar manner.

Because Chinese cabbage is delicate, cut it finely by hand, not in a food processor. I prefer also to cut the red cabbage by hand, discarding some of the stalk, but you could use the processor.

Rather than being mixed together in a bowl, the vegetables are arranged in a pattern, so that each one keeps a separate colour and identity.

You could either serve them individually at the table or toss the entire salad there if you prefer.

It is a good salad to make in large quantities for a party, and good at a barbecue because it combines well with meats.

Serves 8

Salad:

3 cups finely shredded Chinese cabbage
3 cups finely shredded red cabbage
1 white onion, finely chopped
1 large or 2 medium-sized carrots, grated
1 large daikon or white radish, grated
½ **cup alfalfa sprouts**

Dressing:

1 cup vegetable oil (8 fl oz)
1 tablespoon sesame oil
1 clove crushed garlic
1 tablespoon soy sauce
2 tablespoons white wine vinegar

Mix together the oils, garlic, soy sauce and vinegar. Whisk in a bowl, or shake in a jar, until thick. Set aside.

Place all the salad ingredients in separate bowls.

Add half the onion to the Chinese cabbage and the other half to the red cabbage.

Toss both these with sufficient dressing to moisten well and let them stand for 1 hour before using.

About 10 minutes before assembling the salad, add a little dressing to the carrot and white radish.

If the cabbage is not sufficiently moist, add more dressing.

Place the Chinese cabbage in a triangular shape on one side of a platter or wide, shallow bowl. Place the red cabbage, in a similar shape, next to this.

Arrange the carrot opposite the red cabbage and fill the remaining space with the white radish. Mound alfalfa in the centre.

When served it will become mixed, but it looks interesting presented separately when taken to the table.

Cabbage salad with Sesame seeds

A cabbage salad which seems conventional in ingredients is transformed by the addition of sesame seeds, which leave a lovely nutty taste on the palate.

Use a young cabbage for this salad and remove all the heavy stalk before shredding.

This salad is best served with barbecued or grilled meats.

Serves 4

3 cups finely shredded cabbage, firmly packed (about ½ **a small cabbage)**
1 white onion, finely chopped
¼ **cup finely grated carrot**
2 tablespoons sweet-sour cucumber, chopped small

2 teaspoons vegetable oil
2 tablespoons sesame seeds

Dressing:

½ **cup (4 fl oz) vegetable oil**
2 tablespoons white wine vinegar
salt and pepper
1 tablespoon mayonnaise

Very good, except for the onion

Mix the cabbage with the onion, carrot and cucumber. In a frying pan, warm the oil, add the sesame seeds and cook, stirring continuously, until the seeds are golden on the outside. Remove immediately, before they overcook.

Add the seeds to the cabbage and mix with the dressing.

To make the dressing mix the oil and vinegar and season well. Add the mayonnaise and whisk until thick.

Let the salad stand for 1 hour before serving. It can be covered and kept refrigerated for about 6 hours if necessary.

Cabbage salad with Pears and Sultanas

This salad is much nicer than it may sound.

The small quantity of yogurt in the dressing combined with the lemon is fresh tasting, and the pears and sultanas with honey is slightly sweet.

The choice of pears is an important factor in the success of this salad. If they are too ripe they will break easily when the salad is tossed and if they are too hard they will not have sufficient flavour.

This salad is particularly good with poultry.

Serves 4

3 cups finely shredded cabbage, firmly packed (about $\frac{1}{2}$ a small cabbage)
2 medium-sized eating pears
1 tablespoon lemon juice
2 tablespoons sultanas (raisins)
salt and pepper

Dressing:
$\frac{1}{4}$ cup (2 fl oz) yogurt
3 tablespoons vegetable oil
1 tablespoon white wine vinegar
1 teaspoon finely grated lemon rind
2 teaspoons honey

Peel and core the pears and cut into small dice. Mix with the lemon juice and stir to coat the pears.

Add the pears and sultanas to the cabbage. Season with salt and pepper.

Mash the yogurt in a shallow basin and gradually whisk in first the oil, then the vinegar. Stir in the lemon rind and honey. Mix the dressing into the salad, stirring gently so that the cabbage is thoroughly coated but the pieces of pear remain whole. (The pears become soft after a couple of hours so if keeping the salad, add these nearer to serving time.)

Cabbage with Blue Cheese dressing

Marbled with a bluish-green mould, the blue-veined cheeses are among the most intensely flavoured of all.

There are many famous names among these—Stilton, Gorgonzola, Roquefort—and each country has its own particular version.

Only a little needs to be used in the dressing with this cabbage salad to give it a wonderful bite and tang.

It is the sort of dish in which you could use up any leftover pieces of blue cheese, provided they have not dried out or become too bitter.

If I have a choice, I prefer to use a tablespoonful of Roquefort, which is just the right amount. If you try different types of cheese you may need to adjust the quantity but this can easily be done by tasting the dressing and adding more if necessary.

Serves 4

2 tablespoons vegetable oil
1 large onion, cut in half and thinly sliced
1 medium-sized green pepper (capsicum), cut into small strips
3 cups shredded cabbage, tightly packed (about $\frac{1}{2}$ a small cabbage)

Dressing:
1 tablespoon blue-vein cheese
$\frac{1}{3}$ cup ($2\frac{1}{2}$ fl oz) vegetable oil
1 tablespoon white wine vinegar
2 tablespoons mayonnaise

In a frying pan, heat the oil and add the onion and pepper. Sauté, stirring occasionally, until slightly softened.

Mix into the cabbage, with the dressing, and leave to stand for 1 hour.

To make the dressing, mash the cheese and mix in the oil gradually. Add the vinegar and mayonnaise. Taste for seasoning.

You can cover and refrigerate the salad for up to 8 hours before serving.

Jellied Beetroot salad

Although beetroot is always popular, it can be awkward to serve because its bright red colour can so often stain table-cloths and clothes.

By making it in the form of a jelly, it can be cut into slices or small wedges and presented more easily.

It looks lovely made in a ring mould or a round shape, but always serve directly from the refrigerator. Any jellied dish has a tendency to become soft in a warm room and if you compensate by making it firm in the beginning, it won't be as pleasant to eat.

Serves 10

500 g (1 lb) beetroot (beets)
2 teaspoons salt
water
$\frac{1}{3}$ cup ($2\frac{1}{2}$ oz) sugar

$\frac{1}{2}$ cup (4 fl oz) white wine vinegar
1 bay leaf
few peppercorns
1 tablespoon gelatine

Place the beetroot into a pan with water to cover. Add salt and cook, covered, until the beetroot is quite tender. (Check by piercing one with the point of a knife.) Reserve the liquid.

Leave to cool slightly. Under running water, rub the beetroot skins with your hands. They will slip off easily. Cut the beetroot into small dice.

Measure out $1\frac{1}{2}$ cups (12 fl oz) of the reserved liquid and add to this the sugar, vinegar, bay leaf and peppercorns. Simmer gently in a pan for about 5 minutes.

Mix the gelatine with 2 tablespoons of cold water, stirring well so no dry powder remains, and add to the pan. Heat for a moment until it dissolves.

Allow the mixture to cool slightly, but don't leave until cold as it is best poured over the beetroot while still warm.

Place the beetroot into a mould which holds approximately 5 cups (1.25 litres). Strain the liquid into the mould. Season well. Chill until set.

It can be unmoulded and kept covered in the refrigerator for 3 days.

Serve in slices, or, if you prefer, you can make little individual moulds.

Cucumber shreds with Green sauce (page 126)

Jellied Beetroot salad (page 129)

Mixed Shredded salad (page 128)

Marinated Mixed Vegetables (page 126)

Beetroot salad with Onions

The onions should be just warm when placed over the top of the salad so they lend a sweet, rich flavour to the beetroot and lettuce.

However, you don't have to cook them at the last moment. They can be sautéed during the day and gently reheated just before taking the salad to the table.

I prefer to use freshly cooked beetroot for the salad, both for the flavour and so that it can be presented in neat, small dice rather than in slices.

If you want to save time you could use the tinned product, well drained, with each slice cut into quarters before placing them on the lettuce.

This salad is good with barbecued or grilled meats.

Serves 6
3 medium-sized beetroots (beets)
1 cup (8 fl oz) liquid in which the beetroots were cooked
$\frac{1}{2}$ cup (4 fl oz) red wine vinegar
$\frac{1}{3}$ cup (3 oz) sugar
2 medium-sized white onions
2 tablespoons vegetable oil
lettuce
endive

Dressing:
$\frac{1}{3}$ cup (2$\frac{1}{2}$ fl oz) oil
1 tablespoon white vinegar
salt and pepper

Place the beetroots into a saucepan and add sufficient water to just barely cover them. Season with a little salt. Cook until they are quite tender when pierced with the point of a sharp knife.

Remove and leave to cool slightly, until you can handle them. Using your hands, rub the skin to remove it.

Cut the beetroots into small dice and place in a bowl.

Return 1 cup of the cooking liquid to a saucepan, add the vinegar and sugar. Bring to the boil and immediately pour over the beetroot. Leave to stand for 24 hours before using. They will keep in the liquid for several weeks in the refrigerator.

Cut the onions in half and then into wafer-thin slices, the finer the slices the better the flavour in the salad.

Heat the oil and add the onion. Sauté, stirring occasionally, until the onion has softened and is a very pale golden colour. Don't let it darken or the flavour will become too strong. The onion can be set aside and warmed again when finishing the salad.

Arrange about 12 lettuce leaves in a bowl.

Remove the yellow sprigs from some endive and add a small handful of these to the lettuce.

Mix the dressing ingredients together. Add the dressing to the salad and toss lightly.

Drain the beetroot and place on top. Scatter the onion over the beetroot. Don't toss again before serving.

Potato and grated Beetroot mould

Potato, coated with finely grated beetroot, ends up as a salad that ranges in colour from pale pink to bright burgundy but has quite a mild flavour.

The beetroot for this salad should not be the tinned variety; it must be freshly cooked and then grated when it is cool. This should not present any problems, it is just a matter of allowing sufficient time to prepare the beetroot first.

As there is no vinegar in the fresh beetroot it has a light flavour and a finer texture. Using the tinned product will make the salad too strong and sharp.

In other words, don't cheat in this recipe!

Serves 6
500 g (1 lb) beetroot (beets)
500 g (1 lb) potatoes
125 g (4 oz) bacon, cut into small dice
2 hard-boiled eggs, roughly chopped
1 medium-sized white onion, finely diced

Dressing:
$\frac{1}{3}$ cup (2$\frac{1}{2}$ fl oz) sour cream
$\frac{1}{4}$ cup (2 fl oz) mayonnaise
$\frac{1}{2}$ teaspoon dry English mustard
1 teaspoon grated horseradish relish
3 tablespoons vegetable oil
1 tablespoon white wine vinegar
salt and pepper

Place the beetroot into a saucepan. Cover with water, add a little salt and cook, covered, until tender. Remove and leave to cool slightly. Remove the skins by rubbing them.

Let the beetroot cool completely.

Cook the potatoes, in their skins, in salted water. Drain, leave to cool and peel. Cut into dice.

Fry the bacon until crisp and add to the potato. You can add 2 tablespoons of the bacon fat if you wish.

Mix in the egg and onion.

Grate the cooled beetroot on a coarse grater and stir into the salad.

Make the dressing by mixing the cream with the mayonnaise, mustard and horseradish. Stir well. Whisk the oil and vinegar together and add. Season to taste.

Add the dressing to the salad, which will now become pale pink.

The salad can be covered and refrigerated if necessary. It will become firmer in texture but will still taste good.

To serve, pack the beetroot salad lightly into a basin, pressing down gently with a spoon. Turn out on to a platter.

Potato and Pea salad

This is a dish to treasure for one period of the year—the time when the first new potatoes appear, with their fragile, transparent, papery skin and waxy interior, which is perfect for salads.

At about the same time the sweet young spring peas come into season. They make a wonderful combination in a salad—so good it could be eaten as the most important part of a meal, with perhaps a side platter of chicken or thin slices of ham.

It is nicest if it is not refrigerated but served at room temperature within 30 minutes of making.

Serves 4
500 g (1 lb) green peas in
  the pod
1 large sprig mint
2 teaspoons sugar
salt
500 g (1 lb) tiny new
  potatoes

Dressing:
½ cup (4 fl oz) olive or
  vegetable oil
1 tablespoon lemon juice
  or white vinegar
2 teaspoons sugar
salt and pepper
2 tablespoons finely
  chopped parsley
1 tablespoon finely
  chopped mint

Shell the peas, reserving about 6 of the pods. Place the peas and the 6 pods into a saucepan of boiling water, add the mint, sugar and some salt. Cook until just tender. Drain the peas. Remove the pea pods and the mint.

Cook the potatoes, in their jackets, in salted water until tender. Drain and when cool enough to handle peel away the skin. Cut the potatoes in half or into quarters, depending on the size.

Mix the peas and potatoes together gently and add the dressing. Stir.

To make the dressing, mix all the ingredients together in a bowl and whisk them, or shake them in a jar. The dressing shouldn't be too lemony but the flavour will depend on the variety used, so add a little extra if it is too bland when mixed into the salad.

As the salad cools, the potato will absorb some of the dressing. Before serving, stir gently again so the peas and potatoes are well coated.

Potato salad with Olives

A tasty potato salad which has green pimento-stuffed olives, adding both colour and a sharp flavour. Good with meat or chicken.

Serves 4
500 g (1 lb) small new
  potatoes
1 tablespoon vegetable oil
1 medium-sized white
  onion, finely diced
125 g (4 oz) bacon, cut into
  thin strips or small dice
salt and pepper
¼ cup (2 oz) finely chopped
  green pimento-stuffed
  olives

2 tablespoons finely
  chopped chives

Dressing:
⅓ cup (2½ fl oz) oil
1 tablespoon white vinegar
1 teaspoon French mustard
pinch of sugar
1 tablespoon mayonnaise

Place the potatoes, in their skins, into cold salted water, and cook until they are tender. Drain and leave to cool slightly. Peel them and cut into thick slices.

While the potatoes are cooking heat the oil and add the onion and bacon. Cook gently, stirring occasionally, until the onion has softened slightly and the bacon fat is transparent.

Mix this into the potatoes and add the olives and chives.

Mix together the dressing ingredients, stirring well. Add to the salad.

Artichoke and Potato salad

You can use fresh artichokes in this salad but the preparation is lengthy and except for a few rare times in the year they are extremely expensive.

I like it made with the Italian artichokes which come in jars. Spiced and marinated they have a wonderful flavour which blends into the potato.

Another substitute, although not quite as good, is the canned artichokes in brine. Be sure to drain away all the liquid and cut them into small quarters as they are usually in large sections in the tin.

Serves 4
500 g (1 lb) small new
  potatoes
1 cup (approximately) of
  artichoke quarters
3 hard-boiled eggs

Dressing:
1 clove garlic, crushed

½ cup (4 fl oz) olive oil
2 teaspoons French or
  Dijon mustard
2 tablespoons lemon juice
salt and pepper
2 tablespoons finely
  chopped white onion
2 tablespoons finely
  chopped parsley

Cook the potatoes, in their skins, in salted water. Drain and when cool enough to handle, peel them. Cut each into about 5 wedges, as you would an apple.

Place in a bowl with the artichoke pieces and add the dressing while the potatoes are still warm.

To make the dressing, place all the ingredients in a bowl or in a jar and whisk or shake until well mixed.

Toss the salad and leave to stand; as the potato cools it will absorb the dressing.

Cut the hard-boiled eggs into quarters, give the salad a stir, and arrange the eggs on top before serving.

Potato salad with Smoked Salmon and Caviar

Served in a cup of lettuce, this salad has sufficient colour, flavour and presentation to be served as a first course.

As an accompaniment it is best with fish, but you need to have quite a well-flavoured fish or the salad will overwhelm it.

Serves 4

500 g (1 lb) small new potatoes
100 g (3½ oz) smoked salmon
2 hard-boiled eggs, chopped
lettuce
45 g (1½ oz) pink caviar
watercress or parsley sprigs for garnish

Dressing:

2 tablespoons white wine vinegar or lemon juice
⅓ cup (2½ fl oz) vegetable oil
1 tablespoon finely chopped parsley
1 tablespoon finely chopped dill
2 teaspoons finely chopped chives
2 teaspoons horseradish relish
2 tablespoons sour cream
pepper

Cook the potatoes, unpeeled, in salted water. Drain and when cool enough to handle, peel them. Cut into neat dice.

Place in a bowl and while they are still warm, mix with the dressing.

To make the dressing, add the vinegar or lemon juice to the oil, whisking constantly. Add the parsley, dill, chives, horseradish and sour cream and season well with pepper. Don't add salt as there will be sufficient from both the smoked salmon and the caviar.

Leave the potatoes to cool, stirring occasionally.

Cut the smoked salmon into small pieces and carefully stir it through the potatoes. Scatter the chopped egg over the top. Set aside.

When ready to serve, line a plate or bowl with some lettuce leaves. Mound the salad in the centre and arrange the watercress or parsley around the base.

Lastly, just before taking it to the table, carefully spoon the caviar on top as evenly as possible. Serve immediately.

Dutch Potato salad

Although this salad can be eaten several hours after it is made, when the potato has become quite cold, it is at its very best while still slightly warm.

The flavour blends well with ham, some of the spicy or peppery sausages such as a bratwurst, or even simple frankfurts.

Serves 6–8

1 kg (2 lb) small new potatoes
250 g (8 oz) bacon
1 large white onion, finely diced
2 teaspoons sugar
½ cup (4 fl oz) vegetable or olive oil

2 tablespoons white wine vinegar
salt and pepper
2 hard-boiled eggs, roughly chopped
⅓ cup finely chopped parsley

Place the potatoes, unpeeled, into salted water and cook until tender. Drain well and leave them until cool enough to handle.

While they are cooking, dice some of the bacon or cut into thin strips.

Place into a dry frying pan and cook until the fat becomes transparent and the bacon is slightly crisp. Remove to a bowl.

Place the onion into the same pan, using the bacon fat to sauté it, and cook until slightly softened. Mix with the onion.

Add the sugar, oil and vinegar to the pan and cook, stirring well to pick up any little brown crispy bits on the bottom. When it has boiled, pour the liquid over the bacon and onion.

Peel the potatoes and slice them thickly. While they are still warm, toss them lightly with the bacon and onion pieces.

When the salad is cool add the hard-boiled egg pieces and the parsley.

Medley of Vegetables and Fruit in Coconut dressing

This may sound a strange combination but is very good, although better in flavour than appearance because the dressing makes the salad slightly dark in colour.

It can be made and then chilled for 24 hours before eating, if you wish, as it keeps well. In any case it should be left for 3 to 4 hours before serving.

The cooked dressing contains chilli—not enough to make it too hot, just slightly spicy. However, this can be adjusted to suit individual palates. Alternatively, you could use a few drops of Tabasco.

Serves 4

1 cucumber, weighing approximately 375 g (12 oz)
½ teaspoon table salt
1 teaspoon sugar
250 g (8 oz) stringless green beans
½ cup water chestnuts
1 cup fresh pineapple, core removed and cut into small wedges
1 large Granny Smith apple
1 small white onion, finely diced

Dressing:

1 clove garlic, crushed
1 tablespoon brown sugar
2 tablespoons soy sauce
2 tablespoons lemon juice
1 teaspoon finely chopped fresh chilli or few drops Tabasco
½ cup (4 fl oz) coconut milk (see note)

Note: You can either use canned coconut milk or you can make your own from desiccated coconut (see page 60).

Peel the cucumber and score the outside. Cut into wafer-thin slices. Sprinkle with salt and sugar and leave to stand for about 30 minutes, or longer. Drain and squeeze gently to remove the excess moisture.

Cut the beans into small pieces and cook in salted boiling water until just barely tender. Drain and refresh with cold water to retain their colour and prevent further cooking.

Slice the water chestnuts thinly.

Place the cucumber, beans and pineapple into a bowl.

Peel the apple, remove the core, and cut into small dice. Once you add the apple, mix in the dressing.

To make the dressing, place all the ingredients into a small saucepan. Bring to the boil and simmer for about 2 minutes. Leave to cool before adding to the salad.

Add the onion, stir well so that everything is coated with the dressing and leave to stand for at least 3 to 4 hours to marinate the vegetables and fruit.

Waldorf salad

When the Waldorf Salad was first created, its combination of fruit and celery was considered revolutionary. Nowadays fruit in salads is not unusual but this creation by the maître d'hôtel of the Waldorf Hotel in New York caused surprise when it was served at a supper following a benefit concert organised by Mrs Vanderbilt.

Since then, the original simple version has been the base for dozens of different recipes. Some add pineapple, others leave the skin on the apple or remove it, nuts can be added or not; it really can be a dish of personal choice.

The main thing is to have really fresh, crisp eating apples which will retain this quality even when the salad has been standing for a short time. I like to use Jonathan apples, but choose whatever are the best apples in season at the time. Another good choice is Granny Smiths but these need to be peeled because the skin is very firm.

Serves 4

500 g (1 lb) crisp eating apples
lemon juice
1 cup celery, finely diced
2 tablespoons roughly chopped walnuts
½ cup (4 fl oz) mayonnaise
6 lettuce leaves

Garnish:

some additional walnut halves

Peel 2 of the apples and core them. Cut into small neat dice. Leave the skin on the third apple and dice this also. It will add additional texture and colour to the salad.

Squeeze a little lemon juice over the apples and toss lightly so it coats the pieces.

Mix the apples with the celery and walnuts and stir through the mayonnaise.

Chill the salad for about 20 minutes, tightly covered.

Line a bowl with some lettuce leaves. Spoon the salad into the centre and decorate with a few extra walnuts.

Tomatoes with Pesto (page 113)

Salad with Baby Squash and Tomatoes (page 116)

Sweet Carrot salad (page 117)

Marinated Onion salad (page 126)

Salad with Rice, Bean shoots and browned Onions

This is a rather unusual rice salad; the onions gain colour and flavour by being cooked in a mixture of soy sauce, sugar and oil.

It is good served with chicken and, as a variation, you could add fine shreds of carrot.

Serves 4	2 tablespoons pine nuts
1 cup (8 oz) long grain rice	**1 tablespoon sesame seeds**
2 medium-sized white onions	**a little additional oil**
2 tablespoons soy sauce	Dressing:
1 tablespoon sugar	**2 tablespoons vegetable oil**
2 tablespoons vegetable oil	**1 tablespoon lemon juice**
125 g (4 oz) bean shoots	

Cook the rice in a pot of salted water until the grains are just tender. Drain.

Cut the onions into quarters, then into thin slices. Place in a small saucepan with the soy sauce, sugar and oil. Cook gently until most of the liquid has evaporated and they are slightly softened and deep brown in colour.

Pinch and discard the root ends from the bean shoots. Place in a bowl, cover with boiling water and stand 30 seconds. Drain.

Place a little oil in a frying pan and add the pine nuts. Cook, stirring continuously, until they are a deep golden colour. (Be careful, they burn easily.) Place on kitchen paper to drain.

Add the sesame seeds to the same pan and cook about a minute, or until golden.

Mix together the dressing ingredients and stir well.

Mix the rice with the onions, bean shoots, pine nuts and sesame seeds and stir through the dressing. Taste to see if it needs additional seasoning.

Provencale Rice salad

Provence is a region of France noted for a landscape that is carpeted with thyme, herbs and lavender, and an intensity of aromas and flavours in the food which make the simplest dishes in this area more memorable than any sophisticated cooking.

Served with a platter of ham on the side, this Provençale Rice Salad is quite substantial enough for a light meal.

It is best on its own, rather than combined with other salads whose flavours would detract from its lovely simplicity. It is important to use a good olive oil, rather than a vegetable oil, because one of the reasons it tastes so good is the combination of the olive oil with the smoky grilled pepper.

Mix the dressing with the rice while it is still warm so that the flavours will soak in. For the best result, it should be made only a few hours before serving.

Serves 4	(capsicum) (about 750 g
1 cup (8 oz) long grain rice	**(1½ lb) altogether)**
⅓ cup (2½ fl oz) olive oil	**375 g (12 oz) ripe tomatoes,**
2 tablespoons white wine vinegar	**peeled**
1 teaspoon sugar	
4 green or red peppers	**12 small black olives**

Cook the rice in a large pot of salted boiling water until just tender. Drain well.

Whisk the olive oil and vinegar together and add to the warm rice. Season with a little salt and pepper. Toss gently with two forks.

While the rice is cooking, cut the peppers in half and remove the seeds. Press the peppers down with your hand to flatten them so that they can be grilled evenly.

Place the peppers under the griller and grill them until they are blistered and little specks of dark brown, almost verging on black, appear on the skin.

Leave them to cool until you can handle them easily. Pull the papery bits of skin away; if any tiny sections remain, don't worry, they won't spoil the flavour.

Cut the pepper into strips or dice and add to the salad.

Cut the tomatoes into four, squeeze the sections gently to remove the seeds and then dice them.

Sprinkle the sugar over the tomatoes and mix them into the salad, tossing again lightly.

Before serving, scatter the olives over the top.

Broccoli and Macaroni salad

Broccoli is similar to cauliflower in that they are both flowering shoots, but broccoli lends a much more interesting colour to salads.

It is good when picked young and sold fresh; the flavour becomes stronger the longer it is kept. The older plants can be distinguished by the formation of flowers and are tinged with yellow. Broccoli with this appearance would not be suitable for salads (or for cooking, in my opinion).

Cooked until just crisp and yet tender, combined with some toasted pine nuts, macaroni and smoky pieces of pimento, this makes a good accompaniment for plain meat dishes.

This salad could also be served as a simple main course for lunch, with the addition of diced ham or chicken. (Use about 2 cups of either in proportion to the ingredients listed below.)

Serves 6	Dressing:
250 g (8 oz) small macaroni	**½ cup (4 fl oz) light olive oil**
2 tablespoons vegetable oil	**2 tablespoons white wine vinegar**
2 white onions, cut in thin half-slices	**1 tablespoon mayonnaise**
2 tablespoons pine nuts	**salt and pepper**
185 g (6 oz) broccoli	
1 × 240 g (8 oz) tin pimento	

Bring a large pot of salted water to the boil. Add the macaroni. Stir to make sure it doesn't stick to the base. Cook over a fairly high heat until just tender. Drain well. Rinse with cold water for a minute and then leave to drain thoroughly.

To make the dressing, mix together all the ingredients and whisk with a fork until lightly thickened.

Mix the dressing into the macaroni as soon as it has drained.

Heat the oil in a frying pan and cook the onions until slightly softened, stirring occasionally. Add to the macaroni.

There will be a thin film of oil remaining in the pan, return to the heat and fry the pine nuts, stirring continuously, until they are golden brown on the outside. Be careful not to overcook them; they change from white to brown very suddenly. Mix into the salad.

Remove all the flowerets from the broccoli. The smaller the pieces, the nicer the salad. The stalk can be used if it is not too tough but it is improved by peeling. The outside of the stalk will peel away easily, leaving a tender piece in the centre. Cut into several pieces.

Cook the broccoli in salted water for about 5 minutes. It should still be crisp. Drain and refresh under cold running water to retain the colour.

Drain the pimento, cut into small dice and mix the broccoli and pimento through the macaroni.

The salad should be allowed to stand for at least 1 hour before serving, but it can be left all day if you wish. If the weather is warm, place it in the refrigerator, well covered, as broccoli has a strong aroma.

Remove from the refrigerator an hour before serving and mix well again to moisten.

Raspberry vinegar

Dressings

Cooked mayonnaise

Slightly sweet, slightly sharp, this mayonnaise is an old fashioned style which keeps well, uncovered, in the refrigerator for about 1 month. You can make it as suggested in a double boiler or jug, but it can also be made directly in a saucepan providing a whisk is used and it is stirred constantly. It then takes only about 3 minutes. It can boil without harm, as the cornflour stabilises it.

$\frac{1}{3}$ **cup (3 oz) sugar**
1 tablespoon cornflour
  (cornstarch)
2 teaspoons dry, English-
  style mustard
2 eggs
1 teaspoon salt
$\frac{3}{4}$ **cup (6 fl oz) milk**
$\frac{3}{4}$ **cup (6 fl oz) white**
  vinegar
30 g (1 oz) butter

In a jug, beat together the sugar, cornflour, mustard, eggs and salt. Add the milk and vinegar.

Place the butter on top and stand the jug in a pan of hot water, stirring occasionally, until the mixture has thickened. Alternatively, you can cook the mixture in a double boiler.

Oil mayonnaise (opposite)

Oil mayonnaise

With a rich, almost velvety texture and thickness which binds and holds ingredients together, an oil mayonnaise is one of the important basics of many salads.

It can be made by hand with care and a generous amount of elbow action, but also almost equally well in a food processor. There are still many purists who prefer the hand method, but it is sensible to choose the one which you find easiest and which can best fit into your time schedule. It is important to always use a dry bowl; any moisture present will curdle the mayonnaise quickly. It is a help if you warm the bowl slightly first and in winter, thick cloudy oil should be left to stand in its bottle in a sink with a little warm water around it before using. Either a whisk or wooden spoon can be used to make mayonnaise. The oil should be added almost drop by drop at the early stages, then can be added more quickly.

Mayonnaise made in a food processor has a slightly heavier and thicker consistency than that made by hand.

Once made, mayonnaise can be stored in the refrigerator, don't keep an oil mayonnaise too long, although it can be stored, covered, for some days.

If it should curdle during the preparation, there are several ways it can be retrieved. Either place another egg yolk into a fresh bowl and add the curdled mixture a little at a time, whisking by hand. You can also put some Dijon or French mustard into a bowl and add the mixture to this, but it does give a more dominating mustard flavour. It is obvious that the use of olive oil gives a very rich mayonnaise and some people now prefer to use lighter flavoured oils. This is a matter of personal preference, but if you like the olive flavour there is no reason not to use half olive, half peanut oil.

Oil Mayonnaise (1)
2 egg yolks
1 teaspoon French or Dijon
  mustard
pinch salt
$\frac{3}{4}$ **cup (6 fl oz) oil**
1 tablespoon white wine
  vinegar

Mix the yolks with mustard and salt. Gradually add the oil, just a few drops at a time if making by hand, a little faster than this in a food processor. When about $\frac{1}{2}$ cup of oil has been added, mix in the vinegar and then add the remainder of the oil.

Oil Mayonnaise (2)
Because a whole egg is used instead of just yolks, this mayonnaise is slightly lighter in flavour and texture.

1 large egg
1 teaspoon French or Dijon
  mustard
pinch salt
$\frac{3}{4}$ **cup (6 fl oz) oil**
1 tablespoon white wine
  vinegar or
lemon juice

Mix the whole egg with the mustard and salt. Gradually add the oil, a little at a time.

When about half has been added, mix in the vinegar or lemon juice and then add the remainder of the oil.

Dressing with Anchovy

Makes approximately ⅓ cup (2½ fl oz)

1 tablespoon finely chopped anchovy fillets
½ teaspoon dry, English-style mustard
¼ cup (2 fl oz) vegetable oil
or
¼ cup (2 fl oz) olive oil
1 tablespoon white wine vinegar
pepper

Crush the anchovies well with a fork, add the mustard.

Gradually add the oil and then whisk in the vinegar with a fork.

Season with pepper.

Don't add salt as the anchovy will supply sufficient.

Dressing with Egg

Makes approximately ½ cup (4 fl oz)

1 small hard-boiled egg, finely mashed
1 tablespoon capers, finely chopped
1 tablespoon finely chopped sweet-sour cucumber
⅓ cup (2½ fl oz) vegetable oil
2 tablespoons white vinegar
1 tablespoon finely chopped parsley
1 tablespoon finely chopped chives

Mix together the egg, capers and cucumber.

Mix in the oil and vinegar and whisk slightly, using a fork.

Add the parsley and chives.

This dressing can be left to stand for several hours, but stir well before using.

Dressing with Fresh Herbs

Makes approximately ⅓ cup (2½ fl oz)

¼ teaspoon, dry, English-style mustard
¼ cup (2 fl oz) vegetable oil
1 tablespoon white vinegar
2 teaspoons finely chopped parsley
2 teaspoons finely chopped chervil
2 teaspoons finely chopped chives
1 teaspoon finely chopped fresh tarragon

Mix the oil gradually into the mustard. Add the vinegar, whisking so it is thick. Mix in the herbs and whisk again. Stir well before using.

Dressing with Anchovy (opposite)
Dressing with Egg (opposite)

Blue Cheese dressing

Makes approximately ½ cup
(4 fl oz)
1 tablespoon blue cheese
1 tablespoon cream
¼ cup (2 fl oz) vegetable oil
1 tablespoon white wine
  vinegar
pepper
lemon juice (optional)

Mash the cheese to a creamy texture and add the cream. Mix in the oil, vinegar and some pepper.

The flavour, which should be fresh and tart, will depend somewhat on the type of cheese you use. Add a squeeze of lemon juice if you feel it is necessary.

There should be sufficient salt from the cheese so taste the dressing before adding any salt.

Spiced dressing

This should be spiced but not fiery hot. It depends, of course, on the chilli sauce. Brands seem to vary enormously and when trying three different ones recently they all varied between mild and sweet to fire and brimstone.

Add the chilli last and put just sufficient in the dressing to give it a little spice and bite according to your own taste and what you are going to serve with it.

Makes approximately ⅓ cup
(2½ fl oz)
¼ cup (2 fl oz) vegetable oil
1 tablespoon white wine
  vinegar
½ teaspoon paprika
½ teaspoon French or Dijon
  mustard
½ teaspoon chilli sauce

Whisk the vinegar into the oil, using a fork, and add the paprika, French mustard and then the chilli.

Taste for salt, it probably won't need any, depending on how much is in the mustard and chilli sauce.

Anchovy dressing with Olive and Pimento

Makes approximately ½ cup
(4 fl oz)
1 hard-boiled egg
1 tablespoon finely
  chopped parsley
2 teaspoons finely chopped
  anchovy
2 teaspoons chopped capers
2 teaspoons chopped black
  olives
1 tablespoon finely
  chopped pimento
⅓ cup (2½ fl oz) vegetable
  oil
1 tablespoon white wine
  vinegar

Mash the egg and mix in the parsley, anchovy, capers, olives and pimento. Everything should be quite finely chopped to tiny little pieces.

Mix in the oil and vinegar. (The sauce will be thick.)
Taste before adding seasoning.

Blue Cheese dressing (above)

Vinegars

In most of the recipes in this book, a plain wine vinegar is used and additional flavourings are added to each particular dish as needed. However flavoured vinegars have many uses in the kitchen. They can be made into dressings for plain salads, and used in marinades and sauces.

You can steep herbs, vegetables, fruit and even flowers in vinegar to extract and hold their aroma and flavours. Many of the products can be store-bought but it is little work to make your own if you have a herb garden. One herb can be used or a variety can be blended together. Experimenting is part of the fun.

Most vinegars have to be kept for at least 2 to 3 weeks before being used so that the flavours can develop. Some need much longer. It is very much a tasting process as the strength of herbs can vary considerably, depending on their size and the time of year you pick them. But if the vinegar doesn't turn out exactly right, it can be fixed. Too strong and it can be diluted with more vinegar; if not flavoured enough, it can be left to mature for longer or some fresh sprigs of herbs can be added.

You must use glass containers to prepare the vinegars and they should not have any metal contact, even a metal spoon should not be used to stir. If you only have jars with metallic lids, cover the top with plastic wrap before sealing. Bought vinegar bottles have plastic lined tops which are ideal. It is best to place the herbs and vinegar into a wide-necked jar to mature, then strain into narrow bottles. Almost all fresh herbs can be used in vinegar. Pick them before they bloom if you can, since this is when their flavour is at its strongest. Wash well, and leave them to dry on kitchen paper for about 6 hours before using. The only exception is basil, which should be used quickly. The mixture should be left to steep in a sunny place, such as a window sill and turned upside down, shaken or stirred occasionally. Once ready, and judge by tasting, strain carefully through some cheesecloth and then bottle. They can be kept in a cool cupboard for about a year.

Spiced Mint vinegar

There are many varieties of mint, which is one of the most popular herbs of all. Use either spearmint or applemint, which is a rounder leaved variety. Spearmint gives a refreshing flavour, and applemint, as the name implies, combines the flavour of both mint and apples.

$\frac{1}{2}$ cup mint, removed from
   the stalks
6 stalks chives
8 whole black peppercorns
2 thin strips chilli
2 cups (16 fl oz) white wine
   vinegar

Place the mint in a jar with chives, peppercorns and chilli. Add wine vinegar and cover.

Stand in a sunny place for 1 month before using. Strain and add a fresh sprig of mint, chive and some peppercorns to the bottle.

Lavender vinegar

If you are puzzled as to where you could place lavender vinegar in the kitchen, try it with dishes which are to be eaten with lamb.

It is light in flavour but very aromatic. There are different lavenders, English, which is quite strong and has the finest aroma, Dutch, which is similar but comes from a smaller bush and French, which has less fragrance but is a good colour.

The flavour of the vinegar depends on the strength of the type of lavender you use, and how many sprigs you place in the vinegar. You don't want it to be too powerful, so smell the flower and judge for yourself. If the finished product is too strong you can tone it down with some more vinegar, and if it is not flavoured sufficiently, you can always add a few more sprigs.

5 heads lavender, including
   flower, stalk and a couple
   of leaves
2 cups (16 fl oz) white wine
   vinegar.

Place the lavender in a bottle. Cover with vinegar. You must keep the heads under the vinegar so cut the stalks if necessary.

Leave in a sunny place, covered, for 2 weeks before straining. Place 1 fresh sprig of lavender in the bottle before using.

Lemon and Spearmint vinegar

1 lemon
$\frac{1}{2}$ cup roughly chopped
   spearmint, including
   some stalks
2 cups (16 fl oz) white wine
   vinegar

Using a vegetable peeler, remove some of the thin yellow peel from the lemon without taking too much white pith. Place into a container with the spearmint. Add the vinegar.

Stand in a sunny place for 2 weeks, taste, and if strong enough, strain. Otherwise leave for another week.

Tarragon vinegar

The Russian tarragon, easier to grow than the French, does not have the same flavour for making vinegar as the French one. If you use the Russian variety, you will need more than specified in recipe.

$\frac{1}{2}$ cup lightly packed pieces
   of French tarragon
2 cups (16 fl oz) white wine
   vinegar

Place the leaves into a jar and cover with vinegar.

Leave in the sun for 2 weeks, taste and if not flavoured well, leave another week. Strain and place a fresh sprig of tarragon into the bottle.

Borage vinegar

The brilliant blue flowers of borage fade very quickly in vinegar and impart a slight cucumber flavour. Apart from its use in a salad dressing, a teaspoon of this vinegar in a jug of iced water is very refreshing on a hot summers day.

20 borage flowers
2 or 3 small leaves
2 cups (16 fl oz) white wine
    vinegar

Place the flowers and leaves into a container. Add the vinegar and stand in a sunny place for 2 to 3 weeks. Strain.

Garlic vinegar

3 large cloves garlic
2 cups (16 fl oz) white or
    red wine vinegar

Warm a jar by placing into the oven. Don't attempt to warm it by washing in warm water, as even dried there will still probably be some moisture in it.

Chop the peeled garlic roughly and place it into the jar.

Heat the wine vinegar until almost boiling. Pour it over the garlic.

Leave to cool and stand for 1 week before tasting. If not strong enough, leave for another week. Strain and bottle.

Thyme vinegar

It is believed that there are over a hundred varieties of thyme but many of them are used for rockeries or ground cover. The more common garden thyme, a greyish, shrubby bush, or the fine-leafed lemon thyme, are the two best to use in vinegar.

This recipe makes a scented and strong vinegar; you can cut the flavour down later if you wish by adding more vinegar.

$\frac{1}{3}$ cup thyme, cut into large
    sprigs
2 cups (16 fl oz) white wine
    vinegar

Place the thyme into a bottle. Add the vinegar and be sure the herb is completely covered by liquid.

Cover and stand in a sunny place 2 to 3 weeks. Strain. Bottle with a fresh whole sprig of the herb.

Rosemary vinegar

2 large stalks of rosemary
2 cups (16 fl oz) white wine
    vinegar

Place the rosemary into a container and add the vinegar. Stand 2 to 3 weeks in a sunny place.

Strain and place 1 small fine stalk of rosemary back into the bottle.

Basil vinegar

There are two main varieties of basil; the green bush or the larger-leafed sweet basil. However the red or almost purple-tinged basil is most successful in vinegar and gives it a lovely pale rose-pink colour.

$\frac{1}{2}$ cup basil, including some
    stalks
2 cups (16 fl oz) white wine
    vinegar

Place the basil into a container. Add the vinegar and make sure the basil is completely covered by liquid.

Cover and place in a sunny place for 2 weeks, taste and leave for another week if necessary. Strain. Add a whole fresh stalk of the herb to the vinegar.

Celery vinegar

250 g (8 oz) celery
2 teaspoons celery seeds
$\frac{1}{2}$ teaspoon salt
1 teaspoon sugar
2 cups (16 fl oz) white wine
    vinegar

Chop the celery into small dice. You can use the firmer outside stalks for making this vinegar. Put them into a jar or bottle (it is easier to use a container with a wide neck).

Place the celery seeds, salt, sugar and vinegar into a saucepan and bring to the boil. Pour over the celery and leave to cool. Cover and stand for 2 weeks in the sun. Strain.

You can add strips of celery, mainly for appearance if you wish, but this is not necessary for flavour.

Lemon vinegar

1 lemon
1 shallot, chopped finely
2 cups (16 fl oz) white wine
    vinegar

Using a vegetable peeler, cut 3 long strips from the lemon. Be careful not to take much of the white pith. Place into a bottle with the shallot and add the vinegar.

Cover and leave in a sunny place for 2 weeks. Strain. Add a fresh lemon strip and more chopped shallots if you wish.

Raspberry vinegar

This has become a popular vinegar to use, not so much in salads, but in reductions and sauces in lighter styles of cooking. But this vinegar also has another use. A bare teaspoon added to slightly sweetened iced water makes a refreshing summer drink, with a beautiful pastel pink colour.

Raspberry vinegar (1)
250 g (8 oz) raspberries
1½ cups (12 fl oz) white
  wine vinegar

Crush the raspberries lightly with the back of a fork. Add the vinegar and leave in a glass basin or china container for 4 days. It should be kept covered but at room temperature and stirred every day.

Strain, you can press down lightly on the berries when you do this to extract as much juice as possible but don't push any pulp through the sieve. Bottle. Don't use for at least 1 month.

Raspberry vinegar (2)
250 g (8 oz) raspberries
1½ cups (12 fl oz) white
  wine vinegar

This is a cooked vinegar and the flavour, while still tasting very much of raspberry, is a little more mellow. Place the raspberries, crushed lightly, into a china or glass bowl and add the vinegar. Leave to stand, covered, for 4 days. Stir each day.

Strain, pressing down very lightly to extract all the juice from the berries. Place into a saucepan and heat gently. Don't let it boil but simmer for about 7 minutes. Skim the top. Leave to cool and bottle. Don't use for at least 1 month.

Oils

Throughout this book you will find some salad dressings specifying olive oil, others asking for vegetable oils. This is because the rich flavour of olive oil adds to some dishes while in others, a milder oil is preferable.

But rely on your own taste and preference to decide on which one to use: in some cases the best result is obtained by mixing two oils together. The oils specified in the recipes are meant to be merely suggestions and they are the ones we found most satisfactory when testing.

Olive Oil

This oil was used since earliest times and there have been records about it found in parts of Egypt, Palestine and Europe. There is a huge variation in the quality, character and taste of olive oils, depending on their origin, the type of olive which was used, the exact degree of ripeness when harvested and the methods used for extracting the oil. It is sensible to find one which has a flavour that suits not only your palate but also the dish you are making.

Pure olive oil is produced from successive pressings of olives which have been heated to enable the oil to be released. Light in colour, it is not so fine in taste.

Virgin olive oil, or extra fine virgin olive oil extracted by mechanical means but no heat or chemicals are used. This oil may often have a slight greenish-gold tinge.

Olive oil requires good storage conditions. It is affected by heat and by air. It should always have a fruity aroma and flavour, with no waxy or rancid aftertaste. Some oils have such a strong olive flavour that they overwhelm all the other ingredients in a salad. Be cautious and if it is too strong you can blend it with a lighter vegetable oil.

Oils flavoured with Garlic or Herbs

You can buy exotic oils flavoured with herbs or make your own by placing a few whole cloves of garlic or various herbs in the oil and leaving them to steep for several days. Use within 5 or 6 weeks or the oil will become strong and develop a rancid taste.

Chinese Sesame Oil

Used mainly in oriental cooking, it is made from toasted sesame seeds and has a rich nutty flavour. It is quite different from the refined sesame oil available in supermarkets. A little goes a long way so it is best to use a cautious hand.

Safflower Oil

Made from the seeds of the safflower, it is light with a slight nutty flavour.

Sunflower Oil

Made from the seeds of the sunflower, this is a very light, mild oil.

Peanut Oil

Originally this had a strong taste of peanuts but present refining has removed much of the flavour leaving only a light, slightly nutty character.

Walnut Oil

This was once primarily used in Europe by painters for mixing pale colours with white and mainly known in districts where walnut trees were grown. Lately it has become popular for exotic salad dressings and although very expensive it can be obtained in many gourmet shops. The strength can vary, so taste before using as too much can dominate. It does not keep well and is best when fresh.

Hazelnut Oil

A new addition in the shops, it is used in the same way as walnut oil but again, strengths vary according to brands so be cautious. Only use this oil in dishes which have an affinity with the particular nut flavour. At its best it is a very fine oil, but keeping qualities are not indefinite once it is opened.

Grape Seed Oil

Mild and slightly sweet in comparison to other oils, grape seed oil can be used both in salads and cooking. Its advantage over other oils is that it does not spit under normal cooking heat.

Index